IS YOUR GOD REAL?

Timothy E. Crosby

Review and Herald® Publishing Association
Washington, DC 20039-0555
Hagerstown, MD 21740

The author assumes full responsibility for the accuracy of all facts and quotations as cited in this book.

This book was
Designed by Bill Kirstein
Cover photo by Armstrong Roberts, Inc.
Typeset: 11 pt. Palatino

Acknowledgments

PRINTED IN U.S.A.

R & H Cataloging Service

Crosby, Timothy Eugene, 1954-
Is your God real?

1. God (Christianity). I. Title.
231

ISBN 0-8280-0430-7

To the Reader

In light of the increasingly secular mind-set of contemporary society, the author has written this book, on the one hand, for those who do not start with Christian presuppositions and do not believe in the supernatural. Although we cannot prove God's existence, the author has attempted to demonstrate the reasonableness of belief in Him and in His Word and to provide answers for some of the fundamental objections to Christianity, such as the problem of pain. Thus confirmed Christians will doubtless find some of the argument elementary, yet helpful in dealing with those who are not believers. On the other hand, the author uncovers new ground in his examination of certain issues surrounding the nature of God. You will be intrigued, for example, by his unconventional arguments regarding the necessity of law in chapter 3.

The last half of the book deals with the topic of inspiration, tackling such topics as the use of sources, inerrancy, and rules of interpretation. Many Christians find themselves confused over conflicting ways of understanding God's revelation to man. The author has tried to derive an understanding of inspiration from the Bible itself, using both a deductive approach (one that looks at what the Bible claims for itself) and an inductive approach (one that examines the phenomena in the Bible to see how inspiration works in actual practice). The author shows the importance of avoiding either too rigid or too lax a view of inspiration, while retaining a solid faith in and respect for God's Holy Word.

Contents

Chapter 1

God's Existence: How Can We Know?

As soon as our conversation passed from banalities to religion, I discovered that I was talking with the first honest-to-goodness atheist I had ever met. "As far as I'm concerned," he told me firmly, "there is no God. Period." At the time I hardly knew what to say because we shared so few presuppositions.

He owned an electronics shop and worked hard. Wanted to get ahead, he said. He shared a house in an Atlanta suburb with a woman who was not his wife but who had attended my church. Now her way of life concerned her, so she asked me to visit with her friend. I did.

"If you can prove to me that God truly exists, then I'll believe in Him and change my lifestyle," he challenged. We talked for an hour before I began to see that nothing I said would change his mind, for he didn't want to believe. He had too much to lose.

Does God exist? The number of people who doubt His existence seems to have mushroomed since the turn of the century. How do we know God exists?

Perhaps we should begin by tackling a simpler question, like how do we know that Howard Hughes existed? For several years in the mid-1970s people speculated whether or not the famous industrialist, aviator, and movie producer was still alive. For reasons of his own, Hughes chose not to reveal himself except to a select few. The wealthy recluse died in 1976 at the age of 70. Most people believe that Hughes was a real person.

But what proof of Howard Hughes' existence—or that of any other person, for that matter—do we have?

Other than personal acquaintance, the only proof consists of (1) institutions an individual founded, (2) that person's writings, (3) photographic evidence, and (4) the oral or written testimony of those who have encountered the man or woman in question.

God Himself has not written anything except the Ten Commandments (if one believes the biblical account). Jesus Christ wrote only a few words in the sand. Hughes also wrote little. But a name attached to a document doesn't prove much anyway. The document might be a literary forgery.

Howard Hughes is alleged to have founded several large companies, while God is alleged to have created the world, and Jesus Christ is alleged to have begun the Christian religion. But apart from photographic and manuscript evidence, this might be difficult to prove. Giving a company the name Hughes does not prove anything.

So what about pictures?

Thousands of motion pictures bear dramatic testimony to the reality of people and events that never existed. And if a feature film proves nothing, a snapshot proves even less. Pictures can be fabricated, photographs can be altered, and anyone can pose for one under another name.

Besides, we have no photographic evidence at all for individuals who lived prior to the nineteenth century and certainly none for God. Like Howard Hughes, He does not seem to want to be pictured in any way. "You saw no form of any kind the day the Lord spoke to you at Horeb out of the fire. Therefore watch yourselves very carefully, so that you do not become corrupt and make for yourselves an idol, an image of any shape, whether formed like a man or a woman, or like any animal on earth or any bird that flies in the air, or like any creature that moves along the ground or any fish in the waters below" (Deut. 4:15-18).

All the evidence that remains is the testimony of others. And if you think about it a moment, you'll see that the vast majority of facts that we hold to be true (the existence of black holes, the Virgin Islands, and leprosy; or that water is composed of oxygen and hydrogen) are facts for which most of us have no evidence other than the oral or written testimony of someone else.

Thus we have no absolute scientific proof that Howard Hughes ever lived—only secondhand evidence. However, I don't know anyone who denies that Hughes lived, for his existence holds no threat. There is no emotional cost involved in admitting it.

With God the matter is quite different.

In the world today many intelligent people positively deny that God exists, dismissing the testimony of those who claim to have encountered Him. Such hard-core unbelievers we call atheists. It seems to me that atheism is actually a difficult position to defend, because it's just as hard to demonstrate that God doesn't exist as it is to prove that He does. How can anyone be certain that something or someone does not exist? It is one thing to doubt the reality of God (as do agnostics). However, it requires a quantum leap in arrogance to assume, with the atheist, that one can *know* that there is no God. I believe that when it comes to questioning God's existence, the most that honest people can really say is that they have never encountered Him.

Surely even the most intellectually brilliant atheist in the world must admit that he or she knows no more than a fraction of all there is to know about the universe. Right?

Is it not possible, then, that God could exist somewhere in that part of the universe that he or she does not know? By admitting this, the atheist becomes an agnostic. Agnosticism is a much more reasonable position. Agnostics doubt that God exists, though they admit the possibility that they might be wrong.

However, from my perspective, agnosticism is an unstable position. It's like sitting on a barbed-wire fence —as soon as you make a move, you fall to one side or the other. Although one may profess agnosticism in theory, in practice one is either an atheist or a believer. And the vast majority of theoretical agnostics are practicing atheists. They live as if God does not exist.

Unfortunately, we can also say the same of a great many professing Christians, which provides atheists with one of their strongest arguments against the existence of God. The vast majority of people in the world today, regardless of what they may believe about God in theory, act without reference to Him. I am not speaking only of those given to wanton debauchery. Far from being depraved, the practicing atheists of whom I speak may have few vices, may even be gentle and kind, but God occupies virtually no place in their thoughts, their time, or their budgets. Their lives reveal a singular lack of worship (not to be confused with church attendance). The awe they have is not for the sacred, but for success. If they have any religion at all, it does not seriously inconvenience them. Whether or not they profess faith in higher things, their trust actually centers on lower things, such as money. They do not need God.

And just here is the crux of the matter. Only recently have psychologists come to realize how much our practice influences our beliefs. Both agnostics and atheists must admit that their desire to be their own master, to be free to live as they please, provides a strong incentive for rationalizing away the existence of God. It is undoubtedly true that some sincere individuals who would like to find God simply do not know where to look. But many more cannot find God for the same reason that a thief cannot find a policeman. They don't want to meet up with Him.

Since belief in a personal God carries with it such a high price, honest unbelievers will recognize that they probably have a hidden bias against belief. Additionally, it seems the more intelligent they are, the stronger the bias. I admit that this bias may at times work in the other direction for those who lack freedom and power in society and who labor under adverse circumstances. But the intelligentsia tend to be particularly susceptible to an arrogant pride that resists submission and questions all traditions and authority—particularly those that restrict their freedom. It is hard for the rich—in whatever sense—to inherit the kingdom of God (Mark 10:25), since those who enter must become as children (Luke 18:17). In spite of the possibility of infinite gain, people in high society do not respond easily to a religion that teaches that the high will be made low and the low made high (James 1:9, 10; Luke 1:52).

For those honest skeptics who really want to know if God exists, whatever the cost (including the surrender of cherished presuppositions), the following arguments will be of interest. But such arguments can never be conclusive because it is impossible to prove the existence of God—or Socrates, for that matter, though the evidence for God's reality is much greater than that for Socrates. The fact is, however, that in real life we rarely have the luxury of absolute proof. We do not function on the basis of certainties, but probabilities. And some weighty evidence indicates the probability of God's existence.

First of all, we need to sort through several traditional but inadequate proofs for the existence of God.

I'll begin with one aspect of what philosophers call the ontological argument (ontology is the science of being or reality), which Saint Anselm first put forward. (Anselm lived from 1033 to 1109. He was abbot of Bec in Normandy, France, when he formulated in writing the ontological argument. He later became archbishop of Canterbury. He is widely regarded as one of the most original and logically rigorous of Christian philosophical theologians.)

Let me try to simplify Anselm's reasoning. The ontological argument affirms that the idea of God implies a reality behind the concept. Anselm argued as follows: imagine a being so great and perfect that nothing could ever surpass that being in greatness and perfection. So far this "greatest conceivable being" exists only in the mind —and yet there is a still greater being, and that is the same being existing in reality. Therefore such a being than which no greater can be imagined cannot exist only in the mind, but must exist in external reality as well. Many logicians, however, would regard this as merely a play on words. A modern variation on the ontological argument says that God must exist, because if He did not exist, we would never have thought of Him. Alas, the same argument would imply the existence of elves.

Then we have the cosmological argument, which Saint Thomas Aquinas popularized. (Aquinas was an Italian Dominican monk who lived from 1225 to 1274. He became a professor of theology at the University of Paris and wrote a book titled *Summa Theologiae*, generally recognized as the best work of medieval theology ever written.) Again, as with the ontological argument, I oversimplify in trying to get to the essence of the argument.

According to the cosmological argument, everything that is begun must have a cause, as common experience tells us. The universe gives evidence of having been begun, and therefore must be an effect instead of a cause. The cause of any effect must be sufficient to produce the effect. In the case of the universe, the only sufficient and adequate cause is God, who is called both the "First Cause" (and who is uncaused) and the "Prime, or First, Mover" (who is unmoved and unmovable). In Hebrews 3:4 we find a similar line of reasoning: "For every house is built by someone, but God is the builder of everything."

Some people find this line of reasoning intuitively obvious, but others regard it as less than convincing. Our intuition is not always trustworthy, because it rests on our day-to-day experiences, which are extremely limited. Physicists have demonstrated that the universe often functions in counterintuitive ways—ways that seem contrary to common sense. They suggest that the laws of quantum physics, as currently understood, actually allow for something to come into existence out of nothing without any intelligent agent as a catalyst.

Finally, the argument assumes that we cannot account for the existence of the universe except with recourse to some kind of cause. The reality of the universe is therefore not self-explanatory, *but* (and here is the key assumption) the existence of God or a Prime Mover or a First Cause *is* self-explanatory. But is the existence of God any more intelligible than that of the universe itself? If the existence of the universe needs explanation, surely so does the existence of God, which is what the cosmological argument is trying to demonstrate, but which it seems also to assume. So the argument "begs the question" by assuming what it is trying to prove. In other words, if every existing thing has an adequate cause, the same thing must also apply to God. So who caused Him? Must we keep going back infinitely?

The teleological argument (also known as the argument from design or purpose) seems a bit more substantial. It may be one of the oldest—if not the oldest—proofs since it likely has its roots in Plato's belief that there is a mind behind the universe. Such a mind moves the universe and orders it. (Plato lived from 427 B.C. to 347 B.C.

A Greek philosopher, he was an extremely influential thinker. In fact, some of his ideas continue to shape modern thought.) According to the teleological argument, the intricate and purposeful design of the universe indicates an intelligent designer. Paul says that the existence of God is clear to us through what He has made. "For since the creation of the world God's invisible qualities —his eternal power and divine nature—have been clearly seen, being understood from what has been made, so that men are without excuse" (Rom. 1:20).

No amount of explosions in a watch factory could ever produce from raw metal a functioning watch. Evolutionary explanations of the universe leave unanswered some basic questions: How could the eye have evolved over millennia, when it would serve no purpose until fully formed? How could amino acids have combined in the "primordial soup" (or primordial clays) to form life, when the chances of such a thing happening are infinitesimal, even given billions of years?

Unfortunately, even this argument is not quite as strong as it might first appear. Purposeful change and certain types of intelligent order *can* result from natural processes. A simple example: The staurolite crystal may assume the form of a perfect beveled cross that appears to have been manufactured. Another example: Certain chemical reactions produce microstructures that mimic some functions of living things, such as reproduction.

On the other hand, one who believes in God would argue that nature works this way only because an intelligent designer created it to do so. At any rate, it seems to me that this argument raises questions that atheistic presuppositions cannot easily answer.

Another argument for the existence of God is the moral one. Formalized by Immanuel Kant in his book *Critique of Pure Reason*, the moral argument does not presume to prove the existence of God, but "claims that divine existence is a postulate, or presupposition, of the claim of morality upon us." (Kant, a German philosopher who lived from 1724 to 1804, is widely recognized as one of the most brilliant philosophers who ever lived. He argued that we should use the concepts of faith and belief when talking about God rather than the concept of knowledge.) Converted atheist C. S. Lewis popularized the moral argument in his book *Mere Christianity*.

Whenever people say "That's not fair!" or "Come on; you promised," they are appealing to a common standard of morality. They are admitting to the reality of some absolute standards of right and wrong that we all acknowledge. But if there is no God, how could this be true? The existence of moral law (formerly called natural law) implies a lawgiver. Rules do not come from out of nowhere, but imply a rulegiver. Without God we can have no absolute morality. Even an atheist would probably quickly admit that Christian morality is superior to Nazi morality. But that very admission indicates that there is some standard of morality by which we may judge both moralities. And no consistent atheist can admit that.

The only possible moral standards in a godless universe are those imposed by the strong upon the weak, or (to put the best face on it) by the majority upon the minority for the "common good." However, history offers us seemingly endless examples of the capriciousness of the majority. It would be difficult for anyone to maintain that the will of the majority is always right. For example, what if the majority were to vote to annihilate all members of the human race with dark skin? Would that be right? Those who do not believe in God find it difficult to answer such questions, since they cannot admit to any transcendent moral standards of right and wrong.

We encounter still another problem with "common good" morality. If I can get away with it, why should I be concerned about the "common good"? If it were to my personal benefit to torture and murder thousands of people, why should I not do so as long as there is no God?

Here's another way to put the moral argument. Skeptics assert as one of the strongest arguments against the existence of God that the universe is cruel and unjust. But how do they know this? We don't call a line crooked unless we have some idea of a straight line. If the universe is unjust, how do the skeptics know what justice is? When we deny that morality is objective, consistency requires that we regard the idea of justice as a merely human idea. But if that is so, then we can no longer claim that the universe is really unjust. Hence the case against God's existence collapses.

Next is an argument I would call the pragmatic argument. If Christianity is not true, then why does it work so well in the real world?

In September 1975 *Redbook* magazine took a survey of more than 65,000 readers, exploring the relationship between the respondents' lifestyle and beliefs. The results revealed that believers were more satisfied with life and more at peace with themselves than those who did not profess religious belief. They even had a better sex life (which is curious, since many often regard Christianity as the spoiler of sexual freedom). Wouldn't it be strange that a false religion could produce such effective living?

Let us look at one case history of the positive effects of Christianity on a culture. In 1852 a missionary named Snow landed on the island of Kusaie in the Carolines. At that time the island was a place of unspeakable horrors, but Snow committed the language to writing and proceeded to translate the Bible. Years later the American Bible Society printed the entire Bible in the islanders' language.

In his book *The Bible Speaks to You*, Dr. Frances Carr Stifler, public relations secretary of the ABS, tells of a 1940s interview with John Sigrah, the king of Kusaie.

Sigrah reported that no murders had occurred on Kusaie in 60 years, and no drinking in 30. There was no jail, and no divorce.

We could repeat similar stories of scores of islands where Christianity has changed filthy, superstitious head-hunters to happy, clean, smiling Christians. During World War II American soldiers stumbled upon many such places. In fact, such people rescued the late president John F. Kennedy when his patrol boat, PT 109, wrecked in the South Pacific.

The Bible has a strange power—a power that no psychotherapy can ever match.

This is as true in America as in pagan lands. A survey of the occupations of the fathers of individuals listed in *Who's Who in America* turned up the surprising fact that more were pastors than any other occupation.

Now, if Christianity is a false religious philosophy, if Christian ministers labor under a delusion, then why do their offspring brought up in that environment do so extraordinarily well in the real world? How can irrationality be so successful? How can a false system produce such superior minds or such well-adjusted members of society? Why is it that Christian teaching has such great power to bring about drastic lifestyle changes for the better? Why is Christian faith one of the most powerful ways to obtain victory over drugs, alcohol, or tobacco? What other psychology or philosophy could turn a tribe of headhunters into loving, caring people? Obviously something is wrong with the skeptics' assumptions.

Finally we come to the testimony of the thousands of individuals who claim to have encountered God in one way or another. They have seen Him in vision, heard His voice, or have felt His presence in a dramatic way. Many have experienced miracles. We have their written accounts in the Bible and in many other books. Their testimony to the work of the supernatural in their lives involves events that have no natural explanation. It is virtually impossible to read these accounts of miraculous healings, escapes, appearances, etc., and believe that all such people are lying or that they are imagining things. When those who make such claims are, in the main, stable people, not given to delusions in other areas of their lives and who tend not to ingest mind-altering substances, then one must take their testimony seriously. It is hard to discount such consistent behavior over so long a period of history as the result of mass hysteria.

So let's return to our original question about how we can determine the existence of someone or something. The vast majority of our knowledge comes not from personal experience, not from demonstration, but from hearsay. Perhaps more than 90 percent of everything we know we learned secondhand through reading or hearing. And all this we've accepted on faith. Unlike animals, human beings can know and understand that which lies outside the realm of their experience because they accept the testimony of others.

For example, most people know only by hearsay that China exists. If you do not accept the corroboration of others, then you have only one possible way to convince yourself that China exists. You must go there personally. To do this, of course, you must assume that China exists at least to the extent of booking passage on a flight that claims to go there. Furthermore, you must fulfill the conditions of entry into that country (inoculations, passports, visas), whatever they may be.

Yet even after you get there, can you be absolutely certain that the ground you stand on is really China? Can you prove beyond a shadow of a doubt that China truly exists? It is possible that your experience is a grand hoax perpetrated by conspirators who have gone to a great deal of expense to erect the necessary signs, to provide the necessary actors, etc. But as you see the sort of faces and encounter certain landscapes that you have seen in pictures about China, the conspiracy theory begins to appear unlikely.

This is all a parable. No scientific experiment can *prove* God's existence. If you are not willing to accept the testimony of those who have encountered Him, then there is only one way for you to find out if He exists. You need to experience Him yourself. Of course, to do so you must approach Him assuming He is real (for example, through prayer) and according to His rules (you must not expect the Sovereign of the universe to lay aside His way of doing things for you and manifest Himself at your bidding in whatever way you dictate).

Of course, even after your heart is strangely warmed, you cannot be certain that it is not merely a psychological experience—a form of self-hypnosis—unless you have the rare fortune to encounter a direct miracle. But as you discover from the inside the sort of experiences that you have heard described by other Christians, as your life begins to change in ways that you were unable to bring about before, the psychological explanation becomes increasingly unlikely.

And this brings us to the ultimate proof of God's existence: His working in your life.

You would have no doubt about Howard Hughes' existence—or God's—if you knew him personally. No miracle is as good as a personal relationship. Theologian William Barclay tells of a reformed alcoholic who said, "I can't prove that Jesus turned water into wine, but I do know that He changed liquor into food and clothes for my family." God will transform your life if you will let Him.

God has specified a method for finding Him in His Word. First of all, you must be in earnest. "You will seek me and find me," says God, "when you seek me with all your heart" (Jer. 29:13). Of course, to seek Him you must be willing to assume His existence. "And without faith it is impossible to please God, because anyone who comes to him must believe that he exists and that he rewards those who earnestly seek him" (Heb. 11:6). Finally, you must obey. In John 7:17 Jesus says that if anyone is willing to do God's will, he will know whether His teachings are true or false. Again, Jesus said, "I am the light of the world. Whoever follows me will never walk in darkness, but will have the light of life" (John 8:12). "If you hold to my teaching, you are really my disciples. Then you will know the truth, and the truth will set you free" (verses 31, 32). God will reveal Himself to those who obey Him: "If anyone loves me, he will obey my teaching. My Father will love him, and we will come to him and make our home with him" (John 14:23).

To find God, then, means to surrender. And that is why so few succeed. It seems so heavy a price to pay—even though the rewards are infinitely great.

So the answer to the question "Does God exist?" is "How badly do you really want to know?"

Chapter 2

God's Nature: What Is He Like?

Suppose that a colony of ants were to compose a descriptive anthropology of human beings. They might say that *Homo sapiens* can travel unimaginably fast, are tremendously strong, are mighty builders, and can work miracles (to an ant, fire would be a miracle). However, such a description does not even begin to sum up the basic abilities of the human intellect. Ants could have no comprehension of electricity, history, mathematics, or modern communications media. Much of human culture would remain inaccessible to them.

As far as we are beyond the ants, so God is beyond us. We cannot comprehend God in all His fullness. Outside the limits of what He has revealed to us is a vast unknowable immensity. " 'For my thoughts are not your thoughts, neither are your ways my ways,' declares the Lord. 'As the heavens are higher than the earth, so are my ways higher than your ways and my thoughts than your thoughts' " (Isa. 55:8, 9).

Although there is much about God that we cannot know, there is still considerable that we can learn through revelation, for He has told us about Himself in His Word and by analogy, for He created us in His image (Gen. 1:26).

God's Personality and Presence—Scripture teaches that God is omnipresent, that in some sense He is present everywhere at the same time. " 'Can anyone hide in secret places so that I cannot see him?' declares the Lord. 'Do not I fill heaven and earth?' " (Jer. 23:24). "He is not far from each one of us. 'For in him we live and move and have our being' " (Acts 17:27, 28).

This means at least that God is always aware of whatever is going on anywhere. "The eyes of the Lord are everywhere, keeping watch on the wicked and the good" (Prov. 15:3). "Nothing in all creation is hidden from God's sight. Everything is uncovered and laid bare before the eyes of him to whom we must give account" (Heb. 4:13). And He can act upon any point or manifest Himself at any specific locale at any time.

We must distinguish the concept of omnipresence from pantheism, which holds that God is a pervasive essence or vital force present in all things. The pantheistic God is as present in a house of prostitution as in a church, in the center of the earth as on His throne in heaven. He exists equally in flowers and in sewage, in Hitler as much as in Mother Theresa, in Satan as in Christ. And therein lies the problem. Such a god makes no difference and can safely be ignored.

The Bible clearly speaks of God as a personality who reasons, loves, creates, destroys, and commands. That is quite different from the vague, amorphous deity referred to as the "ground of being" or the "all" that we find in Eastern religions and in certain forms of contemporary philosophy. As C. S. Lewis noted, the modern concept of God as nature is extremely attractive:

"Men are reluctant to pass over from the notion of an abstract and negative deity to the living God. I do not wonder. . . . The pantheist's God does nothing, demands nothing. He is there if you wish for Him, like a book on a shelf. He will not pursue you. There is no danger that at any time heaven and earth should flee away at His glance. . . . An 'impersonal God'—well and good. A subjective God of beauty, truth, and goodness, inside our own heads—better still. A formless life-force surging through us, a vast power which we can tap—best of all. But God Himself, alive, pulling at the other end of the cord, perhaps approaching at an infinite speed, the hunter, king, husband—that is quite another matter" *(Miracles*, pp. 113, 114).

God's Power—God is also omnipotent, or all-powerful. Job said of God, "I know that you can do all things; no plan of yours can be thwarted" (Job 42:2). And Jesus agreed: "With man this is impossible, but with God all things are possible" (Matt. 19:26).

So God can do anything *that is not a logical contradiction*. Some things He cannot do, because they are logical absurdities. For example, God cannot create another God who is more powerful than Himself. He cannot do two mutually exclusive things such as make a square triangle or create a stone so big He can't roll it. Nor can He cause something to both exist and not exist at the same time. If God wills one thing, He cannot allow another thing that is contradictory.

This limitation, which theologians include when they talk about omnipotence, is not merely hypothetical. It has some very real and serious consequences. Evidently God could not accomplish His goals for the good of the universe without allowing the terrible evil of pain and suffering to continue for a while. He could not maintain our free will and still prevent sin. Thus He had to choose one or the other. (We'll talk more about this in chapter 4.) But one thing He can do: He can save those who surrender their will to Him. God's omnipotence means that He is mighty to save. If He can create worlds, then He can create in us a new heart.

God's Knowledge—The Bible also indicates that God is omniscient, or all-knowing. "I make known the end from the beginning, from ancient times, what is still to come. I say: My purpose will stand, and I will do all that I please" (Isa. 46:10). "For God is greater than our hearts, and he knows everything" (1 John 3:20). As the Self-existent One, God has no beginning and no end. "From everlasting to everlasting you are God," sang the psalmist (Ps. 90:2). There has never been a time when He was not.

To some minds this raises the question of determinism. If God knows exactly what is going to happen, then does that not mean that our behaviour is determined, our course of action fixed?

Not at all. God's foreknowledge need not influence what happens. Cognition—knowing—is not cause. Anyone can through the miracle of television watch a football game at a distant location without thereby influencing the course of events. It is not unreasonable to assume that God's "technology" is far more advanced, enabling Him to see the future without influencing it.

Imagine an airline passenger flying over a freeway. The passenger, looking down, observes a driver who mistakenly turns up the exit ramp and heads north in the south-bound lane. The driver who is going the wrong way cannot see over the next hill, but the observer can see two cars abreast that are about to crest the hill going south. He realizes that there will probably be a collision, but his knowledge does not determine the course of events. If even we can look into the future in a limited way, it is not unreasonable to believe that God knows the future in an absolute way. But His foreknowledge does not mean that our future is fixed, our choices predestined.

God's Stability—When we look around us, we see a world in flux. Such instability extends even to those institutions on which the survival of society depends—its moral principles. Whether we like it or not, in morals as in dress fashions come and go. As I write, for example, racism is out of fashion and promiscuity is in. The old, the traditional, is passé. The word *new* or the word *improved* on a box of soap is a selling point.

In our society changelessness is not a virtue. But there is One who is eternally changeless. "In the beginning you laid the foundations of the earth, and the heavens are the work of your hands. They will perish, but you remain; they will all wear out like a garment. Like clothing you will change them and they will be discarded. But you remain the same, and your years will never end" (Ps. 102:25-27). God "does not change like shifting shadows" (James 1:17). "Jesus Christ is the same yesterday and today and forever" (Heb. 13:8). We call this the doctrine of immutability.

God's basic nature or character does not alter. Never is He full of love today yet full of hate or even apathy tomorrow. Nor is He true today and false next week, fair today and unjust next month, immortal today and mortal next year.

Thus God is not capricious, but reliable. "I the Lord do not change. So you, O descendants of Jacob, are not destroyed" (Mal. 3:6). God will not renege on His covenant promise. He does not go back on His word. Of course, this means that God is faithful not only to His promise to bless in case of obedience but also to His promise to curse in case of apostasy.

"After you have had children and grandchildren and have lived in the land a long time—if you then become corrupt and make any kind of idol, doing evil in the eyes of the Lord your God and provoking him to anger, I call heaven and earth as witnesses against you this day that you will quickly perish from the land that you are crossing the Jordan to possess. You will not live there long but will certainly be destroyed. The Lord will scatter you among the peoples, and only a few of you will survive among the nations to which the Lord will drive you. . . . But if from there you seek the Lord your God, you will find him if you look for him with all your heart and with all your soul. When you are in distress and all these things have happened to you, then in later days you will return to the Lord your God and obey him. For the Lord your God is a merciful God; he will not abandon or destroy you or forget the covenant with your forefathers, which he confirmed to them by oath'' (Deut. 4:25-31).

Clearly, belief in the immutability of God does not mean that He is unconditionally committed to anyone or anything regardless of circumstances. When circumstances change, so do His tactics. His promises and plans include various contingencies.

Jeremiah clearly states the principle. ''If at any time I announce that a nation or kingdom is to be uprooted, torn down and destroyed, and if that nation I warned repents of its evil, then I will relent and not inflict on it the disaster I had planned. And if at another time I announce that a nation or kingdom is to be built up and planted, and if it does evil in my sight and does not obey me, then I will reconsider the good I had intended to do for it'' (Jer. 18:7-10).

God's promises and threatenings are conditional and depend on the faithfulness of His people. He cannot fulfill promises of blessing to a faithless people, and He will not carry out threats of destruction when people repent. This is exactly what happened when Jonah announced to the inhabitants of Nineveh that they would be destroyed in 40 days. They repented, so God withheld the destruction, much to Jonah's chagrin!

Scripture offers several other examples of God's conditional response. Prophecies of Jerusalem's destruction in the days of Hezekiah did not come to pass when the Jews repented (Jer. 26:19). God rescinded Isaiah's prophecy that Hezekiah would soon die from his present sickness (2

Kings 20:1-6). God promised through Elijah to punish Ahab, then relented when the Israelite king repented (1 Kings 21:17-29).

On the other hand, when God's people backslide, He cannot continue to bestow upon them the promised blessings. Because of Eli's disobedience, God retracted His earlier promise that the priest's descendants would serve the Lord forever: "Therefore the Lord, the God of Israel, declares: 'I promised that your house and your father's house would minister before me forever.' But now the Lord declares: 'Far be it from me! Those who honor me I will honor, but those who despise me will be disdained. The time is coming when I will cut short your strength and the strength of your father's house, so that there will not be an old man in your family line and you will see distress in my dwelling. Although good will be done to Israel, in your family line there will never be an old man. Every one of you that I do not cut off from my altar will be spared only to blind your eyes with tears and to grieve your heart, and all your descendants will die in the prime of life' " (1 Sam. 2:30-33).

God's promise to bring the Israelites into the promised land was not fulfilled to the generation that came out of Egypt. "Not one of you will enter the land I swore with uplifted hand to make your home, except Caleb son of Jephunneh and Joshua son of Nun" (Num. 14:30). Through Moses, God assured the Israelites, "The Egyptians you see today you will never see again" (Ex. 14:13), yet Moses later reported that God was threatening to break that promise if they disobeyed Him. "The Lord will send you back in ships to Egypt on a journey I said you should never make again. There you will offer yourselves for sale to your enemies as male and female slaves, but no one will buy you" (Deut. 28:68).

Does this mean that God changes? No. In fact, it is because He does *not* vary in His essential nature and attitude toward sin that He alters His tactics when His people change their attitude toward Him. Water's unchanging property of always seeking the lowest level makes it constantly alter its course. Sometimes it flows placidly, other times raging and cutting. It is not God who changes, but His children who alter their position relative to Him.

The Bible says God is a "consuming fire" (Heb. 12:29). Now, fire is a good example of something that does not change. It is always hot, never cold. But fire produces paradoxical effects. The same flame that melts wax hardens clay. Depending on our distance from it, fire may produce pleasure or pain. As a result, we have a healthy respect for fire, but we are not afraid of it as long as we remain in the right relationship to it—because then we can count on it to behave in certain ways under certain conditions.

God is like that. The fact that He does not change gives us hope, for the only release from the tyranny of the spirit of the age is the Spirit of the ages. An unchanging God has the same miraculous power to save today as He did in Bible times. He ever stands behind the promises of His Word.

"Change and decay in all around I see;
O Thou, who changest not, abide with me."

God's Society—While it is true that God does not alter, His revelation of Himself may modify from age to age, for He reveals Himself more fully as His people accept the rudiments of revelation. Perhaps the central truth of the Old Testament, foundational to all else, is monotheism. "Hear, O Israel: the Lord our God, the Lord is one" (Deut. 6:4). It took the Israelites hundreds of years to get it straight. Only after the Babylonian exile did they learn to despise idols. Then it was time for the next lesson, which came as a bit of a surprise: God is three in one.

The Old Testament does clearly reveal the doctrine of the Trinity. However, it would have been confusing to tell the Israelites that the one God is somehow mysteriously three after He had just weaned them from polytheism. They might have confused the new teaching with the old polytheism. But there is, of course, an infinite difference. The gods of the pantheon fought, caroused, and schemed against one another. The three members of the Godhead are one in substance, thought, purpose, and action.

That the Godhead consists of a plurality of beings we see an indication of in Acts 7:56, where Stephen sees the Son of man (Jesus) standing on the right hand of God, and in Matthew 3:16, 17, where all three members of the Godhead manifest Themselves separately: the Father in the voice from heaven, the Spirit as a dove, and Jesus in the flesh. Paul mentioned the members of the Godhead separately but in conjunction with one another in 2 Corinthians 13:14: "May the grace of the Lord Jesus Christ, and the love of God, and the fellowship of the Holy Spirit be with you all."

In what sense can these three Beings be one? In John 17:22, 23, Jesus asks His Father that His disciples "may be one as we are one." Genesis 2:24 states that husband and wife become "one flesh" when they are married. It is clear that when speaking of coalitions of multiple beings, the Bible uses the word *one*.

The idea that three can be one may seem contrary to common sense. However, that does not mean it is untrue. Certain scientific experiments have indicated conclusively that light consists of waves, and certain other experiments have demonstrated that it is made up of particles. Now, according to common sense, light cannot be both a wave and a particle. Yet scientists tell us that it is! Contradictions are commonplace in the study of physics, which contains ideas far stranger even than this. And if the microcosm is so strange, perhaps the macrocosm is too.

Intuition is reliable only within our "neighborhood" in the cosmos. It is not trustworthy when applied to God or atoms. If light can be both wave and particle, then why cannot God be both one and three?

Perhaps we can understand the Trinity by analogy with human psychology. In any sufficiently complex being, such as human beings, the psyche is not so much a simple entity as it is separate and sometimes conflicting mental entities. The mathematician at work may act quite differently from the lover at home. The left half of the brain may have different skills and personality than the right half. In extreme cases the separate personas may take the form of Jekyll-and-Hyde-like multiple personalities with different characteristics and even different voices. It is as if two or more people inhabit the same body. Normally, of course, the personality is better integrated. The Bible speaks of double-mindedness as a defect of character (James 1:8). The well-adjusted person has integrity, or oneness. The various subentities of the mind cooperate and blend into one another. The individual is at peace with himself or herself. Similarly, God is one. But since God is not limited to a body, His distinct personas may assume separate forms with separate functions. Thus God is not merely a committee of three separate beings who always agree. He is one, as the two halves of the human brain are one.

In Scripture it is the second and third Members of the Godhead who actually maintain contact with earthlings. Scripture calls the first member of the Godhead the Father and the second member His Son, though this does not imply generation. The third member is the Holy Spirit, a person of pervasive intelligence who speaks through the conscience to the hearts of all humans, wooing, warning, and convicting of sin. The Holy Spirit is the inspiration behind Scripture, and He imparts various abilities to the believer. But it is through the second member of the

Godhead that we learn the most about God, for He came to earth to live as a man to reveal God's nature to us.

God in the Flesh—Certain New Testament writers clearly portray the historical Jesus as God. "In the beginning was the Word," writes John, "and the Word was with God, and the Word was God. . . . No one has ever seen God, but God the One and Only, who is at the Father's side, has made him known" (John 1:1-18). Jesus accepted Thomas' acclamation "My Lord and my God!" (John 20:28). And Hebrews 1:8 states: "But about the Son he says, 'Your throne, O God, will last for ever and ever.' "

In the light of such New Testament evidence, certain Old Testament passages take on new meaning for Christians. "For to us a child is born, to us a son is given, and the government will be on his shoulders. And he will be called Wonderful Counselor, *Mighty God*, Everlasting Father, Prince of Peace" (Isa. 9:6). Micah, in predicting the birthplace of Christ, says that His "origins are from of old, from ancient times" (Micah 5:2). Such language the Old Testament uses only of God: "From everlasting to everlasting you are God" (Ps. 90:2).

Yet Jesus accepted worship: "Then those who were in the boat worshiped him, saying, 'Truly you are the Son of God' " (Matt. 14:33). "Then the man said, 'Lord, I believe,' and he worshiped him" (John 9:38). Yet worship is the prerogative of Deity alone. "Worship the Lord your God, and serve him only" (Matt. 4:10). No man or angel is worthy of worship. When the Roman centurion Cornelius kneeled at Peter's feet, the disciple reprimanded, "Stand up . . . I am only a man myself" (Acts 10:26). And when John the revelator fell at the angel's feet, the messenger from heaven replied, "Do not do it! I am a fellow servant with you and with your brothers who hold to the testimony of Jesus. Worship God!" (Rev. 19:10).

Interestingly, New Testament writers apply to Jesus Old Testament passages referring to Yahweh. In Isaiah

40:3 we read about a "voice of one calling: 'In the desert prepare the way for the Lord; make straight in the wilderness a highway for our God.' " Matthew applies it to the role of John the Baptist, who prepared the way for Jesus. "This is he who was spoken of through the prophet Isaiah: 'A voice of one calling in the desert, "Prepare the way for the Lord, make straight paths for him" ' " (Matt. 3:3). Isaiah refers to Yahweh as a "stone that causes men to stumble and a rock that makes them fall" (Isa. 8:14). Peter also describes Jesus as a stone: "Now to you who believe, this stone is precious. But to those who do not believe, 'The stone the builders rejected has become the capstone,' and, 'A stone that causes men to stumble and a rock that makes them fall' " (1 Peter 2:7, 8).

When Isaiah saw Yahweh seated on His throne, Isaiah exclaimed, "Woe to me! . . . I am ruined! For I am a man of unclean lips, and I live among a people of unclean lips, and my eyes have seen the King, the Lord Almighty' " (Isa. 6:5). John explains that Isaiah uttered those words "because he saw Jesus' glory" (John 12:41).

Jesus shares the titles and attributes of God. As God is styled "King of kings and Lord of lords" in 1 Timothy 6:15, so John the revelator describes the glorified Christ as "King of kings and Lord of lords" (Rev. 19:16). Isaiah records the following words: "This is what the Lord says—Israel's King and Redeemer, the Lord Almighty: I am the first and I am the last; apart from me there is no God" (Isa. 44:6). But in the book of Revelation Jesus tells John, "Do not be afraid. I am the First and the Last" (Rev. 1:17).

God is the Creator (Gen. 1:1; Isa. 44:24), and Jesus is the one through whom God created (John 1:3, 10; Heb. 1:2, 10-12; Col. 1:16).

We might cite many more examples to show that in the New Testament, Jesus occupies the same position that God does in the Old Testament, performing the very same functions. They even share the same throne: "The throne of God and of the Lamb will be in the city" (Rev. 22:3) and "I overcame and sat down with my Father on his throne" (Rev. 3:21).

Other than these explicit claims, what sort of historical evidence do we have that this Man was what He claimed to be?

First, there are His miracles. Modern skeptics who reject their possibility must deal with the fact that even Christ's enemies were unable to deny that He worked miracles. Their only defense was that the miracles must be demonic rather than divine.

Moreover, the miracle stories bear the marks of authenticity. For example, Mark 8:22-26 preserves a curious account of a miracle that proceeds toward success in stages. Christ's first attempt to heal a blind man only partially restores the man's sight so that he sees men "like trees walking." After a second application of power, the healing is complete. Like the cry of dereliction on the cross—"My God, my God, why have you forsaken me?" (Matt. 27:46)—it does not sound like something a writer would invent. Why would Mark recount an imperfect miracle and risk raising embarrassing questions (which are unanswerable even today) unless that is the way it happened? Realism permeates the stories. Note, for example, that after Jesus raised Jairus' daughter, He asked that she be given something to eat (Mark 5:43). And just before this, Jesus had to ask who it was He had just healed (verse 30)! A fabricated Saviour would not have such weaknesses; He would heal perfectly with a touch and certainly not tell the whole world that God had forsaken Him!

Second, we have Jesus' extravagant statements about Himself. "Before Abraham was born, I am," He said (John 8:58). "All authority in heaven and on earth has been given to me" (Matt. 28:18). He even asserted that He had the ability to forgive sins. In light of the exalted claims that

Christ made for Himself, it is foolish, as C. S. Lewis pointed out, to say of Christ, " 'I'm ready to accept Jesus as a great moral teacher, but I don't accept His claim to be God.' That is the one thing we must not say. A man who was merely a man and said the sort of things Jesus said would not be a great moral teacher. He would either be a lunatic—on the level with the man who says he is a poached egg—or else he would be the devil of hell. You must make your choice. Either this man was, and is, the Son of God: or else a madman or something worse. You can shut Him up for a fool, you can spit at Him and kill Him as a demon; or you can fall at His feet and call Him Lord and God. But let us not come with any patronizing nonsense about His being a great human teacher. He has not left that open to us. He did not intend to" (*Mere Christianity*, p. 41).

Skeptics have raised two objections to Lewis's argument.

The first suggests that Jesus was merely mistaken. After all, several other individuals claimed to be the Messiah during this period of Jewish history too. Jesus of Nazareth simply fell into the same trap.

But this argument will not work, for although the Jews were expecting a Messiah, they were not expecting a *divine* one. Their messianic expectations did not include the power to forgive sins, and the claims of Jesus, even when viewed within the context of contemporary Jewish messianic expectations, were not rational at all—unless He was God.

Other figures known to have claimed to be the Messiah, such as Bar Cocheba, never ascribed to themselves, as far as we know, Godhood or the right to forgive sins. In fact, none of the revered founders of other great world religions—Confucius, Mohammed, Buddha—classified themselves as God! Lewis's dictum still stands that any mere human being who makes such claims is on a level with someone who claims to be a poached egg. No one has ever produced an example to the contrary.

The second objection is the assertion that Jesus did not, in fact, actually say He could forgive sins or was God. Such statements, say the critics, are an invention of His biographers. But it is extremely unlikely that Jesus' Jewish biographers would place such statements in His mouth if He never made them. Remember, the Jews did not expect their Messiah to be God. Any Jew would have regarded such claims as blasphemous. Why, then, would any pious Jew make his teacher into a blasphemer by putting such claims into his mouth?

This is not to say that such ideas did not exist in the ancient world. The apotheosis ("elevation to godhood, or deification") of certain figures—Mithra, Asclepius—was indeed part and parcel of certain mystery religions then current in the Roman Empire, and it would not have been surprising if Christianity had come out of this background. But it did not. The surprising fact is that Christianity originated out of Judaism—the most unlikely environment to birth a religion that taught a plurality of the Godhead. The central thesis of Jewish theology is monotheism: "God is one." This is why Judaism rejected Christianity in the end. It could not harmonize Christ's claims with its theology.

Finally, the greatest evidence that Jesus was who He claimed to be is the Resurrection. Something remarkable happened on the first Easter morning. It turned 11 cowering disciples who had hidden themselves for fear of the Jewish leadership (John 20:19) into men who faced those same powerful rulers with bold accusations of treachery. People will not usually proceed with a willful deception at the cost of their lives.

Watergate and Irangate have shown how quickly attempts at cover-up come unraveled in the face of legal penalties. The more than 500 witnesses who saw the resurrected Christ (1 Cor. 15:6) gave the world the highest ethical teaching it has ever known, and lived it in the face of persecution. The chances that a fabrication could motivate such behavior are minuscule.

In the 1850s Simon Greenleaf, a professor of law at the Harvard Law School, wrote *A Treatise on the Law of Evidence*, a standard work in the field that is still in print. In 1846 he decided to use judicial evidence to discredit the validity of the Gospels. After submitting the New Testament accounts to rigorous juridical analyses, he concluded that the Gospels had an impenetrable defense that would hold up in any court of law. And he became a believer. He published his findings in *An Examination of the Testimony of the Four Evangelists by the Rules of Evidence Administered in Courts of Justice* (reprinted in 1965 by Baker Book House).

I believe those who bring an unprejudiced mind to the evidence will reach the same conclusion.

The Ultimate Revelation of God—The incarnation of Christ is a mystery that we cannot fully understand. But because of it, we know more about God than even the angels around the throne did before God revealed His humility. By coming to this world Christ showed us what God is like, answering the great question about Him: Is He friendly? "Anyone who has seen me has seen the Father" (John 14:9). "No one has ever seen God, but God the One and Only, who is at the Father's side, has made him known" (John 1:18). Of course, Christ couldn't answer all possible questions about God, for a finite being cannot completely model the behavior of an infinite one. Christ became an ant, as it were, to show us what God would be like when subject to the laws of ants, though there is infinitely more of Him than an ant can ever understand.

But this much we can grasp: "Though he was rich, yet for [our] sakes he became poor, so that [we] through his poverty might become rich" (2 Cor. 8:9). He willingly laid aside the privileges of Deity and endured infinite humiliation to save us. "Who, being in very nature God, did not consider equality with God something to be grasped, but made himself nothing, taking the very nature of a servant, being made in human likeness" (Phil. 2:6). The drab veil of flesh reveals God not as a proud tyrant, but as a servant of men, master of demons, conqueror of death, provider, lover, and Saviour. That is good news.

Chapter 3

God's Righteousness: Why Is There Law?

If God is all-powerful, can He do anything He wants? Or do certain moral restraints limit Him as they do us? Are there some things God would never do because they would be wrong? True, the Bible teaches that God is infinitely righteous, holy, and just. He does no wrong and His ways are perfect. But could God sin if He wanted to, or is whatever He does right by definition?

The pagan Greek philosopher Plato first discussed this issue. Is something right because a divine being endorses it, or does the divine being endorse it because it is right? If you believe that justice is anything that God declares to be right, you are a kind of *nominalist*. But if you think that God Himself must conform to certain standards of justice, then you are what philosophers call a *realist*. Careful religious thinkers have come down on both sides of the issue.

Pure nominalism virtually amounts to the philosophy that "might makes right." Justice is merely the caprice of whoever holds the ultimate power in the universe—the whim of Mr. Big.

Now it seems to me that if there is no transcendent principle of justice to which even God must conform—that is, if right is whatever God says it is—then God might as well be just the opposite of what He is and be praised for it. In that case the angelic praises of God's justice that we find in such scriptures as Revelation 15:3, 4 are pointless tautology and meaningless flattery. One does not praise a yardstick for its accuracy unless there is a prior standard to which even the yardstick conforms.

Consider this: what is the point of holding a final judgment that invites the onlooking universe to watch the proceedings? The purpose of such a trial is certainly not to enlighten God as to who is to be saved, because God already "knows those who are his" (2 Tim. 2:19). Hence the only possible purpose is to demonstrate to the universe the justice of the proceedings—the purpose of any public trial. And this implies the realist position, for if justice is whatever the judge says it is, then an open trial is pointless. If whatever God does is right, might He, then, in the judgment arbitrarily damn the sinless angels and save the most wicked of men who had never called upon His name?

Not even the most thoroughgoing nominalist would admit such a thing. They would reply that God must at least be consistent with Himself and His previously established principles. But once someone admits that God must conform to at least one transcendent principle—in this case, that of consistency—the person has essentially adopted the realist position. Strict nominalism, on the other hand, would have to maintain the absurdity that if God should choose to be capricious, then capriciousness would be right and consistency wrong.

You can distinguish nominalists from realists by their answers to the following question: Could God have made it right, even mandatory, for His creatures to torture and murder one another at every opportunity? A nominalist will say yes; a realist no.

Both answers are incomplete. The correct answer is: perhaps in another universe, but not in this one. It is possible (I do not think it is probable) that God could have created a very different universe in which murder would have been good. However, the nature of our present universe dictates that murder must be evil—and if God were to command His creatures to murder at every possible opportunity, He would Himself be evil. (Incidentally, this argument does not rule out war or capital punishment, which, according to Scripture, has its place.)

Let me illustrate it with an analogy. If General Motors were to manufacture a car that ran on sawdust, it would be malicious to recommend in the owner's manual that the owner put water in the sawdust tank. Or if it produced a vehicle that ran on water, it would be wrong to urge the use of sawdust. General Motors might have the right to construct any sort of car it chooses, but once the vehicle is manufactured, it has a responsibility to spell out rules that are for the best good of the car.

Likewise, God might have created a different universe with different laws. (It is reasonable to assume that God created the best of all possible universes, but that is not essential to our argument.) But in the universe He did make, it is inconceivable that He would ever make murder a duty. Such a rule would not work in the universe as we know it, because it would result in misery and pain.

God is "obligated" to create, sustain, and govern His creatures in such a way that they can be happy. Obligated to whom? To Himself. God is His own judge and tribunal—His own grand inquisitor. The entity that holds Him accountable is internal, a part of Himself. Just as higher animals have a greater capacity for guilt (which implies a conscience) than lower animals, so God's capacity for moral anguish must be far greater than ours. If He were to do something out of harmony with His own nature, it would produce in Him something infinitely more painful than the worst pangs of conscience you or I have ever known.

God's principles, therefore, do not come from some cosmic oracle outside Himself. No, the oracle is within Him, but it is not free. Once God created the universe and gave it a specific form, not all possibilities remained equally open. Moral laws are not arbitrary. They spring from the very nature of God Himself and are dictated by the structure of the universe. For instance, think of the physical law of gravity. I do not believe that God arbitrarily decided that objects should fall down instead of up. "Downness" is a necessary part of the system that He created. Similarly, the prohibition of murder reflects the very nature of society and God, and so it is with all other moral laws. God is still absolutely sovereign. He might have created a very different universe with different rules, but He could not have laid down different rules for *our* universe and still be good.

So far so good. But if moral laws are so essential to the well-being of the universe, why did God give His creatures the ability to violate them? Wouldn't it have been better if God had made transgression impossible? Why not turn all the dangerous "ought nots" into "cannots"?

One traditional answer to this question is that it would reduce our freedom. But is such an answer convincing? God has obviously curtailed our freedom in many ways. He made us incapable of flying, of reading other people's minds (even when they want us to), and of becoming invisible. Limitations abound. So why not render us incapable of sinning? Most of us would agree that animals cannot sin, so why not human beings? Why must there be rules?

In any conceivable world, there are many things that are possible but forbidden. For example, although the letters of the alphabet can be strung together in a virtually infinite number of ways, the rules of syntax are highly confining, and only a small fraction of the possible permutations are correct and meaningful. One may construct an entirely different syntax and produce a new language, but it is impossible for meaning to exist where there is no syntax—no linguistic protocol—at all. Could there, then, be meaning in a world where all possibilities were equally legitimate and desirable? Would worship, for example, be possible in a world where there was no protocol, and it was just as legitimate to curse the Creator, or to turn one's back on Him, as to praise Him? If there were no difference between love and hate, could there be love? If there were no thirst or hunger, would eating or drinking be pleasant? In any theoretically perfect world where there were no needs, could there be desire? or satisfaction?

Let us approach this problem from the standpoint of the Creator, and imagine ourselves creating a race of nonmoral robots. We would quickly discover that our robots have great potential for damage unless restricted by certain rules. Scientist and writer Isaac Asimov has proposed that we program robots with the following three fundamental rules: (1) always protect humans; (2) always obey humans, except when in violation of rule 1; (3) always protect self, except when in violation of rule 1 or 2. Such rules constitute a primitive "conscience." True, they are programmed into the robot, making it incapable of transgression; hence this is not an "ought not" but an impossibility. But that is only because we are dealing with primitive intelligence. Higher intelligences require manifold and sometimes, conflicting rules of behavior, so the rules must be made conditional and not absolute.

Already we detect the beginnings of free will in the robots governed by Asimov's robotic rules. Note also that even at this primitive level, under certain circumstances the rules come into conflict with each other. That's why they are laid down in a hierarchy so that only the first one is absolutely inviolable. The lower ones are to be observed only under certain conditions and transgressed under other conditions. This is the first step toward what in a more complex creature would manifest itself as free will and moral conscience.

I suggest that such rules must exist in any created world. A universe inhabited by articulate creatures without moral restrictions would be as meaningless as a round square. God made beings with free will and the ability to sin because intelligence on this level requires such freedom. Creatures are not free to love unless they are free to hate. Where blasphemy is impossible, so also is praise.

Since moral laws are necessary, perhaps an examination of some of the principal examples that God has laid down for His creatures will tell us something about God and something about the universe He has created.

God's Law—The Ten Commandments constitute the basis of God's moral law for our world. The usefulness of the last six rules are rather self-evident. Parents can understand that life is better when children obey (fifth commandment). Husbands and wives would not want their spouses to commit adultery (seventh). It is obvious that killing (sixth), stealing (eighth), and perjury (ninth) disrupt society and that coveting (tenth) makes everybody unhappy. The laws of most societies include similar injunctions. But what of those first four commandments that have to do with our duty toward God? How are they relevant to us? They seem a bit self-serving on His part. Why not be generous and let everyone worship whatever god he or she wishes (first two commandments)? Why one day of worship out of seven (fourth)? And why must God be so sensitive about His name (third)? Why be a spoilsport?

In the preamble to the Ten Commandments, God says, "I am the Lord your God, who brought you out of Egypt, out of the land of slavery" (Ex. 20:2). Notice that before God asks anything of His people, He tells them who He is and what He has done for them. "I am your Saviour." God acts first. He delivers from bondage and sets His people free. Only then does He request something from His people in return. He did not say to the Israelites "If you will keep all My commandments, then I will save you from the Egyptians" even though, as their Creator, He certainly had that right. Instead, He first saved them, then asked for obedience in return, which is the same pattern of grace that we find in the New Testament. The common idea that salvation is by law in the Old Testament and by grace in the New is a fallacy, for the law is itself based on grace.

We see, then, that God is a deliverer of the oppressed, a Saviour, a champion. This is God's righteousness. According to the Bible, His righteousness embraces not so much His adherence to a certain set of standards (His rightness), but His saving deeds toward His people (His righting of wrongness). "My mouth will tell of your righteousness, of your salvation all day long, though I know not its measure. I will come and proclaim your mighty acts, O Sovereign Lord; I will proclaim your righteousness, yours alone. Since my youth, O God, you have taught me, and to this day I declare your marvelous deeds. Even when I am old and gray, do not forsake me, O God, till I declare your power to the next generation, your might to all who are to come. Your righteousness reaches to the skies, O God, you who have done great things. Who, O God, is like you?" (Ps. 71:15-19).

After reminding the people that it was He who took Israel out of Egypt, God set about to take the Egypt out of Israel (a much more difficult undertaking). The first thing His people had to learn was that there is only one God and that He is supreme over all the forces of nature. We call such a religion monotheism. A central truth of the Old Testament, it was also a revolutionary principle. For centuries the Israelites had lived in a polytheistic environment in which various supposed spiritual powers and forces competed with one another for the allegiance and the control of humanity. One deity controlled the water, another the trees, etc. The problem was that you could never please them all, and the result was a sense of fear and bondage to the elemental spirits of the universe.

The worship of such gods often involved two major perversions: immorality (sacred prostitution) and cruelty (human sacrifice).

The word *Baal* means "Lord," and Baal was the lord of fecundity—the source of the mysterious power of life and growth. His worshipers believed that he made the corn grow, the grape swell, the olive ripen, and—above all—the child to develop in the womb. With Baal as the source of the power in sex to create life, the sexual act became a sacred act of devotion. Apparently the temples of Baal had crowds of priestesses who were sacred prostitutes. Baal devotees worshiped by having sex with a priestess. Such a religion had a fatal attraction to the lower side of human nature.

Another god, Molech, required his worshipers to throw their children into the fire as a human sacrifice. "He desecrated Topheth, which was in the Valley of Ben Hinnom, so no one could use it to sacrifice his son or daughter in the fire to Molech" (2 Kings 23:10). "They built high places for Baal in the Valley of Ben Hinnom to sacrifice their sons and daughters to Molech, though I never commanded, nor did it enter my mind, that they should do such a detestable thing and so make Judah sin" (Jer. 32:35).

Modern forms of this ancient evil are less superstitious but no less insidious. It is not necessary to invoke the name of some demon god in order to worship at his shrine. The modern versions of such ancient forbidden practices—illicit sex and violence—have come back into style among those devotees of the goddess Cinema. They attend her houses of worship to play the voyeur or derive vicarious pleasure from the portrayal of others' pain. The discotheque, with its orgiastic gyrations, and the bar, with its altered states of consciousness, are other modern variations on those ancient temples or high places that exalted self-indulgence to a virtue.

Another modern god is Appetite. And one of the most successful modern religions, one that is eminently respectable, is materialism, whose millions of devotees worship the god Mammon, or Money. There are many gods and many lords. Dress, music, sports, society, whatever—vanities that come before the One who is, was, and is to come.

The problem with such lesser gods is this: people will inevitably become like the god they worship. Romans 1:21-31 describes the process in some detail. "For although they knew God, they neither glorified him as God nor gave thanks to him, but their thinking became futile and their foolish hearts were darkened. Although they claimed to be wise, they became fools and exchanged the glory of the immortal God for images made to look like mortal man and birds and animals and reptiles. Therefore God gave them over in the sinful desires of their hearts to sexual impurity for the degrading of their bodies with one another. They exchanged the truth of God for a lie, and worshiped and served created things rather than the Creator—who is forever praised. Amen. Because of this, God gave them over to shameful lusts. Even their women exchanged natural relations for unnatural ones. In the same way the men also abandoned natural relations with women and were inflamed with lust for one another. Men committed indecent acts with other men, and received in themselves the due penalty for their perversion. Furthermore, since they did not think it worthwhile to retain the knowledge of God, he gave them over to a depraved mind, to do what ought not to be done. They have become filled with every kind of wickedness, evil, greed and depravity. They are full of envy, murder, strife, deceit and malice. They are gossips, slanderers, God-haters, insolent, arrogant and boastful; they invent ways of doing evil; they disobey their parents; they are senseless, faithless, heartless, ruthless."

When we have nothing higher to worship, we will inevitably slip lower and lower. The ultimate result can assume the form of dark superstition, psychological burn-out, pathological cruelty, or suicide. (Devotees of the god Mammon committed suicide by the scores just after the historic stock market plunge in 1929. Their god was dead, and they had nothing left to live for.)

When we have no point of reference to fix on outside of ourselves, we will worship self, which is not a stable arrangement. When you set a microphone in front of its loudspeaker, the feedback will eventually destroy the microphone. Aim a television camera at its own monitor, and the picture quickly decays into a hallucinogenic vortex, evolving continuously into new patterns of chaos. Those who worship at the shrine of the trivial trinity—me, myself, and I—find themselves caught in an endless spiral into the vortex of self.

God is jealous for our allegiance because He knows what is best for His people. When God says "Put Me first," it is because doing so will produce freedom and happiness. There is a God-shaped hole in our hearts that only He can fill. No lesser deity will fit. As Augustine put it: "God has made us for Himself, and we are restless until we rest in Him."

Hence the fourth commandment. God gives us no choice in the matter of worship. He commands us to cease from our own labors one day a week. Otherwise we would work ourselves to death and forget the One who gives us power to work and reason to live. Psychological studies have shown that one day of rest out of seven is optimal for human health. It is not God's vanity but His mercy that demands our systematic worship. (For further discussion on this commandment, see *A Love Song for the Sabbath,* by

Richard M. Davidson, also in this series.)

But what of the second commandment, which forbids the worship of images? One might think that it is largely irrelevant to us today. We don't worship images. The very idea strikes us as ridiculous. How could sensible people ever pray to a dead, deaf, dumb image? They have their reasons. If you asked an enlightened pagan, he would protest that the image was just a symbol of the spiritual reality beyond—a crutch to help focus the attention. The statue has no power, he would argue. It is merely an aid to worship, just as dolls are useful to teach children how to care for real babies. Of course, this enlightened viewpoint is rare and unstable, quickly degrading into the superstitious veneration of relics on the part of the masses, who don't stop to think what they are doing.

One of the most important tasks of religion is the preservation of awe, which comes only through the constant sense of the transcendent presence of an infinitely great and holy God. The reality of God is as a burning fire. People who recognize that they have to answer to a burning fire will be careful what they do. "Who of us can dwell with the consuming fire? Who of us can dwell with everlasting burning?" asks the prophet (Isa. 33:14). "Our God is a consuming fire" (Heb. 12:29). Fire inspires reverence. The purpose of the second commandment (and the third as well) is the preservation of awe—to preserve the fear of the Lord.

But when the name of the Deity gets debased to an epithet, as happens hundreds of times a day on television, or when His image is degraded to wood and stone, God is trivialized. Wood and stone demand no reverence and arouse no fear. As talismans with some supposed magical power to save, they may give comfort, but they cannot inspire awe. One cannot respect a god who can be dropped in the mud—physically or verbally. So here is the problem. Graven images make for the worst sort of religion there is because they bring a false security without any motivation to holiness.

Images hide more of God than they reveal. When we reduce the eternal Self-existent One who inhabits eternity to a caricature of clay—or even the most magnificent statue—we lose the transcendent and are left with only the physical. And this leads people to forget the transcendent dimensions of their own bodies and glory in the merely physical.

Now we are into familiar territory. Although we twentieth-century people in the Western Hemisphere do not worship images, we are idolaters no less. Our gods have no holiness and demand none, but can be manipulated as a source of personal gratification. Such gods can be made into any convenient image. Society continually revises them to embody the emasculated ideals of the age—love without law, which is merely lust; liberty without self-restraint, which is merely license.

God's laws, then, are for our good. Human happiness depends on living in harmony with them. When we put forth the effort to order our lives according to God's will, we find ourselves in resonance with the cosmos. We experience the harmonies with which all nature sings.

Chapter 4

God's Plan: How Could a Good God Allow Evil?

If, as we have seen, God is angry about sin, then why did He allow it in the first place? Here is perhaps the greatest conundrum ever faced by the human race. Theologians call this the problem of *theodicy*. If God is all-powerful and able to put an end to suffering, and if He is good and detests suffering on the part of His creatures, then why does He allow evil and pain to continue? Many theologians have despaired of a solution. The problem seems to demand that we either deny God's omnipotence or we deny His goodness.

Those who hold to what scholars term process theology tend to deny God's omnipotence. As I understand it, process theology (like Mormonism) affirms that God is in the process of becoming a higher being. Though He is very wise and very powerful, He is neither omnipotent nor omniscient. Since He does not have absolute knowledge of the future, He has limitations just like we do, and He cannot eliminate evil even though He may wish to. Instead, He must be content to win battles here and there, all the while inching toward perfection. A popular presentation of process theology appears in Rabbi Harold Kushner's best-seller *When Bad Things Happen to Good People.*

At first sight, it seems an attractive solution. After all, young children regard their parents as all-wise and all-knowing. Later they come to understand that their parents do, in fact, make mistakes. Is it not possible that the teaching of the prophets about an omniscient God merely reflects religion in its infancy? It is certainly tempting to see in the ins and outs of salvation history a God who is experimenting, trying one thing and, when that doesn't work out, then another.

Such a concept would make it easier to explain those texts that say God changes His mind or regrets certain actions He has taken. "And it repented the Lord that he had made man on the earth, and it grieved him at his heart" (Gen. 6:6, KJV). "And the Lord repented of the evil which he thought to do unto his people" (Ex. 32:14, KJV). "I am grieved that I have made Saul king, because he has turned away from me and has not carried out my instructions" (1 Sam. 15:11). "And when the angel stretched out his hand upon Jerusalem to destroy it, the Lord repented him of the evil, and said to the angel that destroyed the people, It is enough: stay now thine hand. And the angel of the Lord was by the threshingplace of Araunah the Jebusite" (2 Sam. 24:16, KJV). "And he remembered for them his covenant, and repented according to the multitude of his mercies" (Ps. 106:45, KJV). Why should God ever change His plans if He knows everything about the future?

But the limited God of process theology does not sound to me like the unlimited God I read about in Scripture. And if we set aside the God of Scripture, why replace Him at all—particularly when there is another solution to the problem of evil that allows us to retain both God's omnipotence and His goodness.

As I see it, the fatal weakness of process theology is that it provides no solution to the problem of theodicy, one of its alleged reasons for existence. To say merely that God is not all-powerful does not provide a sufficient explanation of the facts of human misery. The question still remains: Why does He not use what power He has more effectively? Why does a God who claims to have the power to raise men from the dead do it so rarely? Surely God is at least strong enough to have prevented Auschwitz—so why didn't He? We must say either that God is grossly incompetent—and thus unworthy of worship and hardly worth bothering about—or that in His infinite wisdom He is doing something the purpose for which may be obscure, but that, though it appears now as an ignominious failure, will ultimately result in glorious victory.

Let us return to the problem of the apparent changes of mind on God's part. Do they imply a lack of knowledge of the future? Not necessarily. The fact that the consequences of an action are regretted does not mean that they were not known in advance. Mary might regret having her dog put to sleep, yet she knew in advance what would happen when she set out for the veterinarian.

Suppose that a well-orchestrated campaign of protest by certain faculty members and students at a university managed to persuade the board, against its better judgment, to make class attendance optional and forgo the use of letter grades. After several years it becomes evident that the scholastic standing of the school has fallen so far that its graduates can no longer get jobs in the marketplace, and enrollment declines precipitously. At this point another campaign results in the restoration of academic rigor. Such a double reversal of policy might not result from a lack of foresight on the part of the board, but in spite of it.

Likewise, it is not unreasonable to assume that God may allow His creatures, if they insist, a certain amount of experimentation to teach them some lesson. The story of one such experiment appears in the biblical book of Job. The story attempts to find a solution to the problem of why bad things happen to good people.

Job is a righteous man who, through no fault of his own, falls upon some very hard times. His children perish, bandits take his property, and he comes down with a painful disease. Then his friends come to comfort him, but end up accusing him of wickedness, since they cannot see why God would so severely punish a righteous man. Though Job protests his innocence, he cannot understand his suffering either. He accuses God of being unfair, and demands an answer. Finally God speaks. The Lord refuses to justify His course of action, but asks Job a number of difficult questions about nature, which the patriarch cannot answer. The implication is that if he cannot understand the ways of nature, how could he understand those of God?

At the end of the book Job repents of his arrogance in thinking to call God to account. His misfortunes reverse, and his prosperity is more than restored. A partial solution to the problem of sin, then, is that at some future time all that is wrong will be made right, all that was lost will be made up for. But while this is good news, it does not solve the problem of why God allowed sin in the first place.

The real answer to Job's experience appears in the beginning of the book, where it takes the reader behind the scenes to a heavenly caucus that Job could not see. Before some sort of cosmic committee, God faces a challenge to prove that His creatures love Him for Himself alone, and not merely for what they get from Him. Satan proposes an experiment: Why not rob Job of all his blessings and see what happens? God accepts the challenge. And as the whole universe watches, our planet becomes a proving ground, a laboratory, and one man enters the crucible of affliction to see if faith will triumph over tragedy in a fallen world.

This one brief glimpse into the "politics" of heaven provides us with a powerful clue toward a solution of the problem of suffering. Somebody is trying to prove a point—a point on which hinges the future safety of all creation for all eternity.

From this and other behind-the-scenes glimpses in the Bible, we can piece together the probable origin of sin. The result is a story that makes sense out of the apparently senseless world in which we find ourselves. It is the ultimate story—all others are footnotes to this one.

Long ago, in the primeval dawn of eternity, before the creation of the worlds, God, through Christ, made a race of majestic creatures, known to us as angels, to love and be loved by Him. Since God could not be satisfied with the fellowship of robots, He gave His creatures free will, like Himself, with the ability to understand and fellowship with Him, and to freely choose to love or not to love. He did so knowing that one day some of them would choose not to love, thus jeopardizing the security of heaven and costing the life of the Son of God.

Sometime, somewhere, somehow, a discordant note began to sound as the sons of God sang together. The highest and perhaps the first of created majesties, the archangel nearest the throne, "full of wisdom and perfect in beauty," whose bidding the other angels delighted to do, began to think strange new thoughts—thoughts he himself did not fully understand. Somehow he became jealous of divine prerogatives, perhaps resentful over the creation of man, which he may have perceived as a threat. He became proud of his wisdom and beauty. His adoration turned inward until the arsenic of self laced every thought.

According to John 8:44, Satan "was a murderer from the beginning, not holding to the truth. . . . For he is a liar and the father of lies." Hints of the story of his fall and subsequent expulsion from heaven appear in Isaiah 14:12-20, Ezekiel 28:11-19, and Revelation 12. According to these passages, Satan began to think the unthinkable. He would usurp the throne of God. Knowing he could never do it alone, he set about to secure the allegiance of the other angels in his rebellion by subtly sowing the seeds of disaffection and doubt. Since he was their leader, and since no one had ever lied to them before, they believed him. Quite possibly he at first believed himself. Slowly he progressed from hints to open accusations. His accusations must have been incredibly clever, for in the end he was able to convince a third of the angels that he was right (Rev. 12:4, 9).

The fact that anyone could induce even holy angels to abandon their loyalty to God shows that even a perfect environment contains room for doubt. An intelligent mind can suggest plausible criticisms of even a faultless being. I imagine that Satan might have said something like this:

"For ages we have sung the praises of God, but now it is time to ask some questions. God is good—as long as we don't cross Him, as long as we consent to be His lackeys, as long as we don't ask any embarrassing questions. But it is all for His own glory and benefit. Is God not a tyrant? He demands of us self-sacrifice, but when has He ever sacrificed anything for us? If you ask Him about all this, He will just say, 'Trust Me.' Does He have something to hide? Why can we not participate in all of the divine counsels? And why are there certain things that we cannot do? He wants us to trust Him. Does He trust us? As exalted and responsible beings, we do not need arbitrary laws to tell us what is right and wrong. He will probably destroy me for telling you this, because He is afraid for you to learn the truth. But if you will support me, I will lead you to freedom."

No doubt Satan's questions were much more cunning than any conjecture we might come up with. Their nature was such that God could not immediately disprove them. To what act of self-sacrifice could He point? How could He convince them that the freedom that Satan offered was, in fact, bondage? How could they understand something they had never experienced? Only by faith.

Eventually war erupted in heaven—a war not of swords or guns, no doubt, but of arguments and ideas and their inherent spiritual powers—and God had to cast Satan out (cf. Luke 10:18) along with the third of the angels that chose to side with him. "His tail swept a third of the stars out of the sky and flung them to the earth. . . . And there was war in heaven. Michael and his angels fought against the dragon, and the dragon and his angels fought back. But he was not strong enough, and they lost their place in heaven. The great dragon was hurled down—that ancient serpent called the devil, or Satan, who leads the whole world astray. He was hurled to the earth, and his angels with him" (Rev. 12:4-9). Satan usurped authority over our planet from Adam (Gen. 3) and became its ruler. Jesus refers to him as the prince of this world: "Now the prince of this world will be driven out" (John 12:31). The fallen angels, originally created perfect beings by God (Col. 1:16), became the occult rulers and authorities of darkness, the spiritual forces of evil mentioned in Ephesians 6:12. We call them demons.

Now for the crucial question: Why did God allow sin to continue and to spread to our world? Why didn't He simply destroy the rebels?

If He had, it would have been an admission of defeat—proof that their questions were unanswerable, and that He was indeed a tyrant. From that moment on, the angels would have served out of fear, not out of love, and the doubts raised in their minds would have festered until some new rebel arose. Once the seeds of sin had been planted, they had to be allowed to grow and bear their poisonous fruit before they could be plucked up. God could have destroyed the rebel, but not the rebellion. Until disproved, ideas are more or less immortal. No doubt even the loyal angels had some unanswered questions, and such lingering doubts could be put to rest only through an acceptable demonstration of their falsity.

A loving God had no legitimate alternative available but to let sin run its course and show its true nature. On the other hand, a God of pure reason, without emotion, might have solved the problem by instantly annihilating the universe and starting all over again. But no loving father, if one of his children got sick with a contagious disease, would deal with the problem by killing the child and conceiving another to take his place, even if it were legal—and God loves His children more than we love ours. Besides, that would have been an admission of failure, and the same thing might have happened to the next batch. God had a responsibility to the creatures He had brought into existence and wanted to save as many as He could.

Obviously God could not simply abolish all law and allow His creatures to do whatever they pleased, thus turning order and harmony into anarchy and chaos. Whatever laws there are exist not for God's benefit but for His creatures,—just as the instruction manual that comes with a new car is for the aid of the owner, not the automobile manufacturer. We have already seen that God's law is not arbitrary, but derives from and is based on the nature of the universe He created. The law—and the penalty for violating it—is immutable.

So God took the hard way out: He chose to allow sin to continue for a time—at infinite cost to Himself. He gave Satan time to prove his claims against God and to demonstrate his system of government. When Adam and Eve accepted the bidding of the serpent in Eden, they chose Satan as their ruler, and our earth became the laboratory of the cosmos, the lesson book, the test of Satan's ideas, for us as well as all unfallen intelligences. "We have been made a spectacle to the whole universe, to angels as well as to men" (1 Cor. 4:9). God intended that "through the church, the manifold wisdom of God should be made known to the rulers and authorities in the heavenly realms" (Eph. 3:10). "Even angels long to look into these things" (1 Peter 1:12). By allowing the germs of sin to infect one planet, God inoculates the universe. By permitting the disease to fester here, He makes the rest of His creation immune by showing sin for what it really is.

The decisive turning point in the great battle between God and Satan was the Incarnation. "The devil has been sinning from the beginning," writes John. "The reason the Son of God appeared was to destroy the devil's work" (1 John 3:8). God came to earth in the person of Jesus Christ to show His creatures what God was like in a human environment, and to provide a way of escape for them from sin. Since the Lord could not fully answer Satan's charges in heaven, where He could not suffer, He came to meet them on earth. While Satan said, "I will ascend" (Isa. 14:13), the Creator announced, "I will descend" (Phil. 2:6-8) to share fully in the suffering of My creatures.

Having lived a sinless life demonstrating what humanity could be by God's power, Jesus died as a perfect sacrifice. At the cross He won the decisive victory in this war. Having assumed human nature, Christ became the second Adam, succeeding where the first had failed. His unique status qualified Him to provide vicarious atonement for His creatures—that is, to pay the penalty for their sins. As the head and representative of the race, He stood in their stead. Yet as the Creator, His life was infinitely greater in value than those of all His creatures. Thus His death could atone for them all.

Theologians have suggested many theories and models to explain the atonement. All of them open up some useful window on the truth, yet none of them reveal more than a fraction of the whole. Some of them stress the aspect of a transaction or substitution required to meet the demands of law, emphasizing that Christ's death somehow satisfied the need for public justice. Other theories portray the atonement as primarily a revelation of God's self-sacrificing love to His creatures. The atonement did all of this and more. No one analogy is adequate.

In fact, I will venture to add a new one: the gambit theory of the atonement. In chess one can often turn a losing position into a winning one by a daring sacrifice —that is, by allowing the opponent to capture a piece. Before he became world chess champion, Bobby Fischer, at age 14, once sacrificed his queen—the most powerful piece on the board—and went on to win what chess experts have called the "game of the century." One of the most powerful openings in chess goes by the term "queen's pawn gambit," involving the sacrifice of the queen's pawn.

The atonement was a shocking, unexpected, and unthinkable gambit (who would have imagined that the Source of life would die?) that could have been devised only by infinite wisdom and infinite love. Such an unspeakable sacrifice not only left God in a winning position with the enemy; it provided for our salvation as well. Christ died the death that was ours that we might have the life that was His. He took our shame that we might share His glory. Who can explain this? It remains an infinite mystery whose depths we will perhaps never fully plumb.

Thus the power of love triumphed over the love of power. Satan and his minions were disarmed: "And having disarmed the powers and authorities, he made a public spectacle of them, triumphing over them by the cross" (Col. 2:15). "Since the children have flesh and blood, he too shared in their humanity so that by his death he might destroy him who holds the power of death—that is, the devil—and free those who all their lives were held in slavery by their fear of death" (Heb. 2:14, 15). Christ reconciled all things to Himself—including heavenly beings. Through Christ God reconciled "to himself all things, whether things on earth or things in heaven, by making peace through his blood, shed on the cross" (Col. 1:20). When Satan dared to crucify the Son of God, he showed himself for what he really was—a liar and a murderer whose system brought not freedom but suffering and death to the innocent and guilty alike. Thus he lost whatever sympathy he might have had among the angels. Eventually, "when the times will have reached their fulfillment," God will "bring all things in heaven and on earth together under one head, even Christ" (Eph. 1:10).

We cannot be sure why God has allowed sin and suffering to continue for so long after the cross. Perhaps human beings themselves have not yet learned some essential lesson. But someday the issues will have been demonstrated to the satisfaction of all concerned.

There will be a public judgment. "And I saw the dead, great and small, standing before the throne, and books were opened. Another book was opened, which is the book of life. The dead were judged according to what they had done as recorded in the books" (Rev. 20:12). "For we must all appear before the judgment seat of Christ, that each one may receive what is due him for the things done while in the body, whether good or bad" (2 Cor. 5:10).

This public judgment will reveal every secret, every obscure purpose. "For there is nothing hidden that will not be disclosed, and nothing concealed that will not be known or brought out into the open" (Luke 8:17). "Therefore judge nothing before the appointed time; wait till the Lord comes. He will bring to light what is hidden in darkness and will expose the motives of men's hearts. At that time each will receive his praise from God" (1 Cor. 4:5).

This judgment will finally vindicate God's justice, and the redeemed will at last proclaim: "Great and marvelous are your deeds, Lord God Almighty. Just and true are your ways, King of the ages. Who will not fear you, O

Lord, and bring glory to your name? For you alone are holy. All nations will come and worship before you, for your righteous acts have been revealed" (Rev. 15:3, 4). At the conclusion of the judgment every living creature—even Satan—will bow before God's throne. Then and only then, when even Satan himself admits he is wrong, will it be safe to destroy sin and sinners.

What we have outlined gives meaning to so much that is otherwise unexplainable. In particular it clarifies the silence of God, the apparent impotence of His cause in the world. If the "great experiment" was to be a fair one, God had to give Satan a rather free hand to develop his principles, thus limiting divine interference in earthly affairs. Brute force would never prove God right. Thus in the battle between good and evil, God voluntarily fights, so to speak, with one hand tied behind His back. In their contest for human souls, both sides find themselves largely confined to working through their human agents. Strictly rationed, miraculous interventions usually occur only in response to united prayer, and may possibly open the door to allow the other side to work countermiracles.

Thus miracles are rare. The entire Bible, which covers a time span of at least 1,500 years, records only about 40. Moreover, they are not evenly distributed throughout, tending to cluster at pivotal points in salvation history. To see a miracle, you have to be in the right place at the right time.

It is not that God has grown weary with the world. His mercies are new every morning. But He has imposed certain restraints upon Himself. Some Christians find this concept threatening to what they perceive to be God's rulership. But if the Lord is truly sovereign, then He certainly has the right to limit Himself. Too much direct interference in the "great experiment" would prejudice its results. God must give Satan a fair chance, and the universe must see what happens when the Lord does not interfere. Again and again He has withdrawn Himself, as He did with Job, to let evil run its course. For example, 2 Chronicles 32:31 says that when the Babylonian emissaries came to inquire about Hezekiah's experience, God left him to himself as a test to see what he would do. Similar examples appear in Exodus 16:4; Deuteronomy 8:2; Judges 2:22; and 3:1-4. Obviously such tests do not benefit the One who knows every heart, but the onlooking universe.

Although at present God is largely silent, the still small voice of His Spirit still speaks to those whose conscience remains sensitive enough to hear. Those who ignore that voice would not respond to more dramatic measures.

We might wonder why God does not remove all doubt by speaking from heaven with thunderous voice to His children. Well, He did that once, at Mount Sinai, only to have His children lapse back into the crudest heathenism a few days later. Raw fear does not motivate for long. When the threat vanishes, it loses its effect. Only one day after God had miraculously opened up the ground to swallow Korah, Moses' accuser, the people brazenly charged, "You have killed the Lord's people" (Num. 16:41).

Jesus' miracles only hastened His execution. Miracles are no cure for unbelief. "If they do not listen to Moses and the Prophets, they will not be convinced even if someone rises from the dead" (Luke 16:31).

And we tend to forget that where God shows Himself, where He is quick to save, He must also be quick to judge. The more light, the more liability. "From everyone who has been given much, much will be demanded; and from the one who has been entrusted with much, much more will be asked" (Luke 12:48). So where there are more miracles, there is more retribution, as with Israel in the wilderness. When God, through Peter, healed the sick, He also promptly slew the dishonest (see Acts 5:1-11). Therefore out of pity for us He often chooses to remain silent.

Lest His glory blind, in mercy He withdraws Himself.

But we are in good company. Even the holiest of men have found themselves forced at times to cry "My God, my God, why hast thou forsaken me?" And though silent, God is not absent. He is there, hidden in darkness, working out His mysterious plan for the good of those who love Him.

We may not understand God's working, but we can trust Him. He has lofty plans for us. One day the redeemed will sit on Christ's throne (Rev. 3:21)—the very thing that Satan desired to do but could not. Already God has "raised us up with Christ and seated us with him in the heavenly realms in Christ Jesus, in order that in the coming ages he might show the incomparable riches of his grace, expressed in his kindness to us in Christ Jesus" (Eph. 2:6, 7).

Chapter 5

God's Word: The Bible

We have been looking at what God has revealed about Himself. Now we will examine the channel that He has chosen to communicate with His creation: the Bible.

It is probably the best-selling, most studied, and most translated book of all time. Few other books have inspired such intense love or hate. Because of it, millions have died, yet at the same time it has relieved the suffering of millions of others. A child can grasp its stories, yet its depths tax the intellect of the wise. The Book's themes and narratives have inspired much of the world's art. It causes proud men to tremble, and fearful men to trust. Hundreds of thousands of books have attempted to explain it, yet its mysteries still tantalize some of the world's greatest minds.

The Bible claims to determine humanity's eternal destiny. "Therefore everyone who hears these words of mine and puts them into practice is like a wise man who built his house on the rock" (Matt. 7:24). "There is a judge for the one who rejects me and does not accept my words; that very word which I spoke will condemn him at the last day" (John 12:48). It has power to give everlasting life. "For the bread of God is he who comes down from heaven and gives life to the world" (John 6:33). It consigns those who disagree with it to outer darkness. "To the law and to the testimony! If they do not speak according to this word, they have no light of dawn. . . . Then they will look toward the earth and see only distress and darkness and fearful gloom, and they will be thrust into utter darkness" (Isa. 8:20-22).

Judging by its history and its claims, the Bible is a dangerous book. One can expect such power of a book that offers itself as the inspired Word of God. Either the Bible is the greatest fraud of all time, or all that it claims to be. Either way, we must seek to understand it.

Why a Bible? The Need for Inspiration—Imagine yourself a passenger on a plane forced to crash-land in a large clearing in the middle of a thick tropical forest in South America. The surviving passengers have no idea where they are. Various trails lead away from the clearing into the jungle in many different directions. Unknown to the survivors, one of the trails will take them to safety in a small village six miles away. The rest disappear into the jungle or end up at the villages of headhunters.

Now, it is possible that left on their own, a few of the survivors might take the right trail and find safety, but their chances would increase greatly if someone were to fly over and drop them a map to show the way.

Just so, God has given His children a map to help them understand the world He has made and its moral laws. It points out to them the way from sin and death to salvation. We call it the Bible. That man needs such a map is painfully obvious. Has human intelligence been able to solve the problems of crime, hatred, pollution, poverty, disease, and pain? A God of love would not allow His creatures to continue in such trouble without providing for them a way out and telling them about it. Since the world in its wisdom was not able to find God (1 Cor. 1:21), He sought us and has revealed Himself to us in His Word.

Why should God's revelation take the form of a book? Why does He not speak to each of us individually? We might as well ask, "Why does God not cause food to materialize on each man's table?" or (to take another tack) "Why don't generals give orders directly to each soldier without going through channels?" God works according to certain rules. Man's sinfulness has cut him off from direct communication with God. However, we do find a few rare exceptions. There are men and women whom God specially chose and prepared to receive His messages. Such individuals recorded their revelations in writing for the benefit of all. It is true that through nature and conscience, God speaks directly to us in a general way. "For since the creation of the world God's invisible qualities—his eternal power and divine nature—have been clearly seen, being understood from what has been made, so that men are without excuse" (Rom. 1:20). "Indeed, when Gentiles, who do not have the law, do by nature things required by the law, they are a law for themselves, even though they do not have the law, since they show that the requirements of the law are written on their hearts, their consciences also bearing witness, and their thoughts now accusing, now even defending them" (Rom. 2:14, 15).

But such testimony is unclear because sin has perverted nature, and our minds are darkened, unable to discern intuitively between the true and the false. Furthermore, without the Bible we would have no standard of truth to refer to whenever people disagreed about what God was saying to them.

Human reason is a gift of the Creator, but unaided, it is incapable of understanding God's will for humanity. He has to tell us some things that at first do not appear to make sense. But the same is true in the relationship between human parents and their children. Children may reason out many things about their world, but there are certain aspects that even the most brilliant of them can learn of only from their parents. When it comes to the question of origins, for example, revelation is required. All of us need more information than reason alone can provide.

But the Bible is not a systematic theological treatise. Basically it is a history book that bears testimony to God's dealings with His people. Its fundamental message is "This is what God is like and how He acts in various situations; here is the plan of salvation He made for you, and here is how to take advantage of it." Furthermore, it is an anecdotal account, for the center of our faith is not some abstract doctrine or teaching, but a living Person. It is not the Bible that is the way, the truth, and the life, but the Christ of whom it speaks. The purpose of Scripture is to lead men to Christ.

History of the Bible—The Bible is a compilation—a library, really—composed by more than 40 authors during a period of some 1,600 years. The Old Testament authors wrote in the ancient Hebrew and Aramaic languages. Jews still consider the first five books, the Torah, as the most holy of inspired writings. They served as a standard to which the writings of later prophets had to conform. Gradually over the next 1,000 years the prophetic and historical books joined them. Isaiah mentions "the law [the books of Moses] and the testimony [the later writings]" (Isa. 8:20) as the standard of truth in his day. Around 500 B.C., after the Jews had returned from exile in Babylon, Ezra compiled many of these documents into a single collection. A few later writings expanded the collection.

Then for 400 years the prophetic Spirit remained silent, producing no inspired writings, although some valuable religious literature (the Apocrypha and pseudepigrapha) appeared during this period. The death and resurrection of Christ in A.D. 31 marked a revival of the work of the Holy Spirit in the world. The New Testament, composed in Greek within the second half of the first century A.D., basically covers the life of Christ and its significance for us today. It was only about this time that the canon of the Old Testament finally became fixed—that is, God's people made a determination as to which books belonged in this authoritative collection and which did not. The canon of the New Testament remained fluid until several hundred years later.

In a book written over so long a period of time by so many different authors of different cultures and languages, we would expect a great diversity of doctrine. Yet the Bible demonstrates an amazing unity in its teachings that points to a Master Designer behind the whole. If we asked 40 different contractors to manufacture parts for a modern airliner and then discovered that the parts fit perfectly into a unified whole, it could only mean that a single intelligence oversaw the matter. Thus the unity of Scripture bears witness to its divine Author.

What the Bible Says About Itself—The Old Testament prophets who spoke in the name of the Lord frequently began their message with a "Thus saith the Lord." They did not choose to be prophets. God selected them—sometimes against their will. Nor did they originate the messages they bore. "No prophecy of Scripture came about by the prophet's own interpretation. For prophecy never had its origin in the will of man, but men spoke from God as they were carried along by the Holy Spirit" (2 Peter 1:20, 21). It was not a personal opinion that prompted what the prophet wrote. He simply communicated the message he or she had received from the Lord. In 1 Thessalonians 2:13 Paul said he was thankful that the members at Thessalonica accepted his message "not as the word of men, but as it actually is, the word of God, which is at work in you who believe." Again in 1 Corinthians 14:37 he emphasizes that his command is God's command.

"All Scripture is God-breathed and is useful for teaching, rebuking, correcting and training in righteousness, so that the man of God may be thoroughly equipped for every good work" (2 Tim. 3:16, 17). Christ said, "Scripture cannot be broken" (John 10:35). God's Word is binding, and it is eternal (1 Peter 1:23-25).

Of course, any book can argue that it is inspired. But how do we know this is true? Let us examine the Bible's claims critically and see if there is any evidence to support them.

In chapter 1 we discussed the Bible's ability to change lives. In chapter 8 we will touch on the subject of its advanced scientific knowledge. Here we shall examine one of the strongest claims of Scripture: the ability to predict the future.

"Remember the former things, those of long ago; I am God, and there is no other; I am God, and there is none like me. I make known the end from the beginning, from ancient times, what is still to come. I say: My purpose will stand, and I will do all that I please" (Isa. 46:9, 10; cf. 44:7, 8).

The Evidence of Fulfilled Prophecy—One of many remarkable fulfillments of Bible prophecy appears in its predictions about the city of Tyre. Tyre was already about 2,000 years old when in 587 B.C., Ezekiel brought God's message of doom against it:

"Because Tyre has said of Jerusalem, 'Aha! The gate to the nations is broken, and its doors have swung open to me; now that she lies in ruins I will prosper,' therefore this is what the Sovereign Lord says: I am against you, O Tyre, and I will bring many nations against you, like the sea casting up its waves. They will destroy the walls of Tyre and pull down her towers; I will scrape away her rubble and make her a bare rock. Out in the sea she will become a place to spread fishnets, for I have spoken, declares the Sovereign Lord. She will become plunder for the nations, and her settlements on the mainland will be ravaged by the sword. Then they will know that I am the Lord. . . . They will plunder your wealth and loot your merchandise;

they will break down your walls and demolish your fine houses and throw your stones, timber and rubble into the sea. . . . I will make you a bare rock, and you will become a place to spread fishnets. You will never be rebuilt, for I the Lord have spoken" (Eze. 26:2-14).

The coastal city of Tyre was quite extensive, stretching for some distance along the shore. Offshore was a well-fortified island to which the citizens sometimes retreated to withstand attackers. Tyre was a city, not of warriors, but of merchants. Known for its trade and commerce, it furnished both material and craftsmen for the building projects of David and Solomon (1 Kings 5:1ff.; 9:10ff.). About the same time that Prince Ahab of Israel married Jezebel, a Tyrian princess, the city founded Carthage on the coast of Tunisia, which eventually grew so powerful that it almost toppled Rome. Through its many exports—including slaves—Tyre became extremely wealthy. The city's wealth aroused the jealousy of several powerful rulers, who repeatedly besieged and forced it to pay tribute.

In 585 B.C., just after Nebuchadnezzar had captured Jerusalem, he turned his sights on the commercial center Tyre. For 13 years his forces surrounded the city, and finally they conquered it—but not before the Tyrians had moved themselves and their treasures out to the offshore island. When the city fell, Nebuchadnezzar found little of value left (Eze. 29:18). But the deserted coastal city fell into ruin, never to be rebuilt, just as the prophecy stated.

For another 240 years the Tyrians continued to ply their wares around the Mediterranean world. However, Tyre still had a date with destiny, since the last part of the prophecy against it still remained unfulfilled. Young Alexander the Great, after marching into Asia Minor and conquering the supposedly invincible Persians at the Battle of Issus, proceeded down the coast of Palestine to Tyre in 333 B.C. By stratagem he attempted to gain access to the city, asking permission to offer sacrifice with his bodyguard to their deity Melquath within the city walls. The inhabitants refused him entrance. Since Alexander had no fleet, he decided to build a causeway from the shore to the island. To do so, he had to collect the abundant stones, timber, and rubble left from Nebuchadnezzar's devastation of the city and throw them into the sea, just as Ezekiel had predicted. After seven months of hard labor his men completed the causeway. Alexander launched a concerted attack with both amphibious forces and an army that marched over the causeway. According to Diodorus Siculus, Alexander killed 8,000 Tyrian defenders in the assault and crucified another 2,000 after taking the city. His forces sold 30,000 women and children into slavery. Although Tyre continued to exist, it had lost all military and commercial importance. It became—and remains today—a place for fishermen to spread their nets on the rocks.

Ashkelon is another city mentioned in Bible prophecy. Listed in Egyptian texts as early as 1800 B.C., Ashkelon stood at the height of its power about the time of Christ. Yet centuries before, Zephaniah had predicted that it would be "left in ruins" (Zeph. 2:4). "Ashkelon will be deserted," Zechariah insisted (Zech. 9:5).

The birthplace of Herod the Great, the city was a center of Hellenic scholarship. Centuries later it played an important part in the Crusades. It certainly looked like Zephaniah's prediction would be a false one. But in 1270 Sultan Beibars crippled Ashkelon, fulfilling the prophecy. *Encyclopedia Britannica* describes the place this way:

"Its now desolate site, on the coast of Israel 12 miles north of Gaza, occupies a rocky amphitheater including about three fourths of a mile of shore with traces of a harbor in the southwestern area. From the sand-swept terrain shattered columns and remnants of ruined buildings testify to former greatness. The site is plentifully supplied with wells, and vines, olives, and fruit trees flourish in the fertile coastal plain."

Bible prophecy speaks against several other cities, such as Tyre's neighbor Sidon (Eze. 28:20ff.) and Jerusalem, yet does not predict complete and final destruction. They still exist today. Scripture declares that the kingdom of Egypt would continue to exist, but only as an insignificant power (Eze. 29:15), and that the disobedient Jews would not be completely destroyed (Lev. 26:44), but would be scattered among the nations of the earth (Deut. 28:37).

Yet the prophets announced the total destruction of other even more powerful kingdoms, such as the Assyrian capital Nineveh (Zeph. 2:13) and the Chaldean capital Babylon (Isa. 13:19, 20; Jer. 51:26, 37). Although they flourished as world powers at the time of the prophecies, today these cities have vanished. How were the Old Testament prophets able to know which powers would merely wane and which would totally disappear? How did Isaiah know that long after Babylon had vanished (Isa. 13:20), the Arabs would still exist and would still live in tents but would superstitiously refuse to pitch their tents on the ruins—as is the case today?

Such prophecies represent only a few of the many examples of Scripture's ability to predict the future. We have not even touched on the numerous Messianic prophesies that predicted the birth of Christ.

Converted Critics—In spite of such evidence, critics of the Bible are quick to pick fault and impute error on dubious grounds. For example, many commentaries still repeat the charge that Esther 2:5, 6 makes Mordecai one of the original captives of Nebuchadnezzar, an impossible situation, when, in fact, it is obvious that it was Kish, his great-grandfather, whom Nebuchadnezzar took into exile. The historicity of Scripture narratives has come repeatedly under challenge, and again and again the science of archaeology has vindicated them. This is not to say that we have no unsolved problems (we will deal with some of them in chapter 8), but the essential accuracy of every part of the Old and New Testaments has been amply confirmed—and often by the critics themselves!

In 1881 Sir William Mitchell Ramsay, a young man of integrity and culture, had come to believe that the Bible was unreliable as a result of his education. Having decided to debunk the history found in the New Testament, he spent years preparing for an exploratory expedition into Asia Minor and Palestine. He decided to retrace the journeys of Paul, using the book of Acts as a guide, thus showing that the narrative was fictional. An honest scholar, though, he vowed to publish whatever his findings might be.

After 15 years of travel and excavation, in 1896 he wrote the book *St. Paul, the Traveler and the Roman Citizen*, which, to the dismay of the skeptics, vindicated the trustworthiness of the book of Acts. "The narrative never makes a false step," he writes (p. 238). Ramsay went on to write a commentary on the seven churches of Revelation that is still a classic work on the topic.

Other men have had similar experiences, such as German scholar Adolf Deissmann, who wrote *Light From the Ancient East*, and General Lew Wallace, an unbeliever challenged by famous agnostic Robert Ingersoll to write a romance on the life of Christ, painting Him as a mere man. Wallace set out to do so, but in the course of his investigations in the Gospels, he found himself forced to the conviction that Christ was more than a mere man. He became a believer and bore witness to his new convictions in his novel *Ben-Hur*.

Unfortunately, many do not bring the spirit of candid investigation and open-mindedness to the Scriptures, and therefore do not arrive at the same conclusions. There is a reason for this. No book has ever received such examination, dissection, testing, criticism, or analysis as the Bible has. Thousands of scholars have devoted their lives to its study. The results of their investigations fill vast libraries. Yet in spite of the wealth of information that supports the authenticity of Scripture, often such study does not lead to faith or moral behavior—it does not change lives, for the investigators do not bring an attitude of humility and submission to the text, but of intellectual pride. Instead of allowing Scripture to stand in judgment on them, they judge it. They regard it not as the word of God to them, but as an object of study, an interesting collection of ancient stories and beliefs. What a sad irony! For one to invest one's life in the analysis of the Bible as nothing more than a work of ancient religious literature is like a group of scientists who, lost in a desert and dying of thirst, stumble upon a sign that points to water one mile away, and decide to go no farther until they have subjected the signpost to extensive scientific analysis to determine its age and authenticity.

Like the sign in the desert, the Bible points to Christ, in whom we find the water of life. Water is to be drunk, not weighed and measured. "Taste and see," says the psalmist, "that the Lord is good" (Ps. 34:8). It is not through logical analysis but through believing in, submitting to, and living by Scripture that men discover its power. Scripture has a transcendent dimension that defies analysis, but that is evident to every sincere reader. The words contain a living power that kindles the spark of hope in the soul. New life is available to anyone willing to receive it on its own terms. Try it and see.

Chapter 6

God's Messenger: Ellen G. White

It is not so hard for us to come to terms with the ancient prophets. Their teachings have become part of the ecclesiastical status quo, and we have grown comfortable with them. We forget the wrenching effect their messages had upon the culture of their day. But when a new prophet comes along and threatens our complacency, human nature rises up in opposition. All down through history God's people have built monuments in honor of the ancient prophets while stoning contemporary ones. It's not so hard to believe the old prophets. The test is to accept the new ones.

One solution to the discomfort of new revelation is to deny the legitimacy of all modern prophets. Many Christians believe that the Spirit of prophecy is silent today. Revelation cannot arise outside of the Bible. Though Jesus said, "I have much more to say to you, more than you can now bear" (John 16:12), some assume that about 70 years later He would say to a now-omniscient church, "I have nothing more to say to you; you know it all." But we have no warrant for the belief that God removed the gift of prophecy from the church after the close of the New Testament.

Some have used Revelation 22:18 to support such a belief, but actually this verse threatens anyone who would delete or add verses to the book of Revelation itself. (The phrase "the book of this prophecy" [KJV] refers to John's own book; cf. Rev. 22:18 with Rev. 1:3.) Sometimes scribes added explanatory notes to a text as they copied or translated it, and several contemporary apocalyptic works—1 Enoch, for instance—are known to have suffered such editing. John did not want this to happen to his book. Revelation 22:18 could not refer to the Bible, for the New Testament canon had not yet been compiled into a book. Each New Testament author's work circulated independently as a separate document, and Christians did not refer to the whole as a book until centuries later. Revelation 22:18 no more prohibits additional inspired writings than does the similar injunction in Deuteronomy 4:2.

The Bible actually predicts the revival of prophecy in the last days. According to Joel 2:28-32, God would pour out the Spirit of prophecy on both men and women, and signs in the heavens would accompany it. The prophecy began its fulfillment on the day of Pentecost (Acts 2), although that by no means represented the complete culmination; for the account mentions no daughters prophesying at that time (in Bible times women frequently served as prophets: Miriam, Deborah, Huldah, Anna, and the daughters of Philip), and we find no record of signs in the heavens.

The New Testament indicates that all of the gifts of the Spirit, including the more spectacular ones of prophecy and tongues, will remain in the church until it is perfected in unity. "It was he who gave some to be apostles, some to be prophets, some to be evangelists, and some to be pastors and teachers, to prepare God's people for works of service, so that the body of Christ may be built up until we all reach unity in the faith and in the knowledge of the Son of God and become mature, attaining to the whole measure of the fullness of Christ" (Eph. 4:11-13). First Corinthians 13:8-12 implies that the latter will vanish only when the perfect comes, which the passage defines as the time when we "see face to face" in the new age. Not until Christ comes will prophecy cease.

The book of Revelation indicates that the gift of prophecy would comprise part of God's true church down near the end of time. Revelation 12:17 says that the remnant, or last part, of God's true church (represented by the pure woman in this chapter) would have two distinctive characteristics: they would keep the commandments of God, and they would have the testimony of Jesus. Revelation 19:10 defines the testimony of Jesus as the Spirit of prophecy. Those who have the Spirit of prophecy are prophets (cf. Rev. 22:9), and Jesus speaks through them to the church. In other words, the gift of prophecy would continue to be manifested within God's church.

According to Scripture, we should not reject claims to prophetic authority without careful investigation. "Do not put out the Spirit's fire; do not treat prophecies with contempt," wrote Paul. "Test everything. Hold on to the good" (1 Thess. 5:19-21).

John agreed: "Do not believe every spirit, but test the spirits to see whether they are from God, because many false prophets have gone out into the world" (1 John 4:1).

The church must expect to meet both true and false prophets, and must learn to distinguish between them. To reject all prophecy would be to "put out the Spirit's fire." "Have faith in the Lord your God and you will be upheld; have faith in his prophets and you will be successful," Scripture says (2 Chron. 20:20).

Prophecy Today—We have a special advantage in understanding how inspiration works because we have a recent example of its operation in the life of one Ellen G. White (1827—1915). She wrote more than 100,000 pages of inspired, Christ-centered material to the church, becoming the most translated woman author and the most translated American author of all time (117 languages).

Her writings—devotional, doctrinal, historical, and practical—contain advice on Christian living, parenting, ministry, administration, and many other matters. Experts have acclaimed her writings on health and education as being years ahead of her times. This is particularly impressive in light of the fact that she had only an extremely limited education. Even famed biblical archaeologist William Foxwell Albright recognized that Ellen G. White fit the Bible pattern of a true prophet (*From the Stone Age to Christianity,* 3rd ed., pp. 18, 19).

Holding herself to be inspired in the same way that Isaiah or Paul was, Ellen White claimed divine authority for her teachings that put them on a different level from the writings of other great Christian leaders:

"When I send you a testimony of warning and reproof, many of you declare it to be merely the opinion of Sister White. You have thereby insulted the Spirit of God. You know how the Lord has manifested Himself through the Spirit of Prophecy. Past, present, and future have passed before me. I have been shown faces that I had never seen, and years afterward I knew them when I saw them. I have been aroused from my sleep with a vivid sense of subjects previously presented to my mind and I have written, at midnight, letters that have gone across the continent, and arriving at a crisis, have saved great disaster to the cause of God. This has been my work for many years. A power has impelled me to reprove and rebuke wrongs that I had not thought of. Is this work of the last 36 years from above or from beneath? . . .

"You might say that this communication was only a letter. Yes, it was a letter, but prompted by the Spirit of God, to bring before your minds things that had been shown me. In these letters which I write, in the testimonies I bear, I am presenting to you that which the Lord has presented to me. I do not write one article in the paper, expressing merely my own ideas. They are what God has opened before me in vision—the precious rays of light shining from the throne" (*Selected Messages*, book 1, p. 27).

How can we determine whether such claims are valid? Unfortunately, there exists no one simple prophetic litmus test. But Scripture gives several criteria that a true prophet must meet. Let us look at the evidence and see if Ellen G. White passes them.

A Virtuous Life—In Matthew 7:15-23 Jesus told how to distinguish between true and false prophets: "By their fruit you will recognize them." Even false prophets can sometimes work miracles (verse 22; cf. Matt. 24:24; 2 Thess. 2:9; Rev. 16:13, 14), but a true prophet will live a holy life adorned with the fruits of the Spirit listed in Galatians 5:22ff., and will engender similar virtues in his or her followers.

This does not mean that prophets have no faults. Peter denied his Lord. The psalmist was a murderer and an adulterer. Though his writings are in the canon, Solomon heeded the advice of false prophets and went after other gods (1 Kings 11:4ff.), which was contrary to the test of Deuteronomy 13:1-3. Again we must repeat that there is no single decisive litmus test. A true prophet might make a mistake, but his or her life will not be characterized by sin or selfish gain.

Throughout the 87 years of her life Ellen White was a pious, self-sacrificing Christian. We find no scandals, no periods when she was missing and unaccounted for, no difference between the public figure and the private one revealed in her voluminous correspondence. For most of her life Ellen White's home was open to a constant procession of visitors who needed food and lodging. She raised a number of orphans. Feeling a special burden for the poor, she gave them cloth for dresses or articles of furniture, asking them if they knew Jesus. Having donated her rather substantial royalties from her many writings to missionary work and charity, she left no wealthy estate to her heirs. Her counsel guided her followers in the development of the largest Protestant educational system and the largest Protestant medical system in the world, not to mention the denomination's extensive welfare and humanitarian activities. The fruits of this tree are good.

Miracles—Although miracles are not a decisive test, because they can be counterfeited, yet God often works them through His inspired spokespersons to validate their message (Ex. 4:1-9; 1 Kings 17; 2 Kings 2; Acts 5:12-16; 2 Cor. 12:12; Heb. 2:4), though not always (John 10:41). Often such signs occur more frequently at the beginning of the prophet's career and diminish over time (1 Sam. 10). In the years following his conversion, Paul's remarkable healing powers (Acts 19:11) diminished later to the point where he could not even heal his own coworker (2 Tim. 4:20). Once the signs have served the purpose of establishing the prophet's authority, they tend to disappear gradually.

Ellen White manifested some remarkable visionary phenomena that followed this pattern. Early in her life she had many public visions. During them she did not breathe (cf. Dan. 10:17), an event confirmed many times by curious onlookers who held a feather, a mirror, and even a lighted candle close to her nostrils to detect any sign of respiration. On one occasion while she was in vision a diehard skeptic actually pinched her nose and mouth shut firmly for half an hour. She suffered no ill effects.

During vision her eyes remained open (cf. Num. 24:4), yet she was unaware of her surroundings. She would faint as she went into vision, but would then be supernaturally strengthened, so that her graceful gestures in vision could not be resisted even when several strong men took hold of her arms to restrain them. During her early years she was instrumental in the instantaneous healing of several individuals. Later her public visions and miraculous healings disappeared, the last public vision occurring in 1884. She continued to have visions at night.

Fulfilled Prophecy—A true prophet is not a soothsayer who spends much of his time predicting the future to satisfy the curiosity of his followers. Instead, he is a spokesperson who brings God's message to the people. The basic message of a true prophet is not usually one of ease, flattery, and comfort, but rather of rebuke, exhortation, and a call to a higher standard. Frankly, a prophet is a nag and a nuisance, often unpopular in his own community. "Jesus said to them, 'Only in his hometown, among his relatives and in his own house is a prophet without honor' " (Mark 6:4). "The Lord, the God of their fathers, sent word to them through his messengers again and again, because he had pity on his people and on his dwelling place. But they mocked God's messengers, despised his words and scoffed at his prophets until the wrath of the Lord was aroused against his people and there was no remedy" (2 Chron. 36:15, 16).

For this reason, Ellen White, like others whom God called to prophesy (Ex. 3; Isa. 6; Jer. 1; 20:9), was reluctant to accept the Lord's commission. In her second vision God showed her that her labors would meet with opposition. "For several days, and far into the night, I prayed that this burden might be removed from me, and laid upon someone more capable of bearing it. But the light of duty did not change, and the words of the angel sounded continually in my ears, 'Make known to others what I have revealed to you.' . . . I coveted death as a release from the responsibilities that were crowding upon me" (*Life Sketches*, pp. 69, 70). Throughout her life she bore the unpleasant duty of rebuke and reproof. In 1874 she wrote, "I have felt for years that if I could have my choice and please God as well, I would rather die than have a vision, for every vision places me under great responsibility to bear testimonies of reproof and warning, which has ever been against my feelings, causing me affliction of soul that is inexpressible. Never have I coveted my position, and yet I dare not resist the Spirit of God and seek an easier position" (letter 2, 1874). Being a prophet is not a glamorous profession.

But although true prophets do little predicting, knowledge of the future is a sign of a true prophet. "You may say to yourselves, 'How can we know when a message has not been spoken by the Lord?' If what a prophet proclaims in the name of the Lord does not take place or come true, that is a message the Lord has not spoken. That prophet has spoken presumptuously. Do not be afraid of him" (Deut. 18:21, 22). "The prophet who prophesies peace will be recognized as one truly sent by the Lord only if his prediction comes true" (Jer. 28:9).

Unfortunately, this is not a foolproof test, for, according to Jeremiah 18:7-10, God sometimes changes His plans when people alter their behavior. Prophecy is not unconditional. "Therefore, O king, be pleased to accept my advice: Renounce your sins by doing what is right, and your wickedness by being kind to the oppressed. It may be that then your prosperity will continue" (Dan. 4:27). Jonah's 40-day prophecy against Nineveh went unfulfilled (Jonah 3:4, 10). Likewise with certain prophecies of Elijah (1 Kings 21:17-29), Nathan (2 Sam. 7:1-17), Isaiah (Isa. 38:1-6), Jeremiah (Jer. 33:18-22), and Paul (Acts 27:10, 22). But a true prophet will not make repeated predictions that prove false.

Ellen White wrote books that contain a substantial amount of prophecy; for instance, the final portion of her historical work *The Great Controversy* portrays the future events on our planet until the final destruction of sin and sinners. She foresaw the 1906 San Francisco earthquake: "Not long hence these cities will suffer under the judgments of God. San Francisco and Oakland are becoming as Sodom and Gomorrah, and the Lord will visit them in wrath" (*Evangelism,* pp. 403, 404). On January 12, 1861, three months before the first gun fired at Fort Sumter, when few seriously expected a long bloody war, she had a vision at a church in Parkville, Michigan, in which she was shown that several of the families worshiping there that day would lose sons in the war, which turned out to be the case. Her 1885 prediction of the ecumenical movement (*Testimonies,* vol. 5, p. 449; *The Great Controversy,* p. 588) is most impressive in light of the strong anti-Catholic sentiment at the time.

One sign of a prophet is supernatural insight into the intimate details of events of which they have no natural knowledge (2 Sam. 12:7; 2 Kings 6:8-14). Such phenomena happened many times in Ellen White's ministry. For example, on June 11, 1887, she sent a letter (letter 30, 1887) from Norway to the business manager of an Adventist sanitarium in California about his improper conduct with one of the female employees there. The man did not admit to any wrongdoing. So a few months later she wrote again and described the intimate details of his infidelity as she had witnessed them in vision:

"A voice said, 'Follow me, and I will show you the sins that are practiced by those who stand in responsible positions.' I went through the rooms, and I saw you, a watchman upon the walls of Zion, were *very* intimate with another man's wife. . . .

"She was sitting on your lap; you were kissing her, and she was kissing you. Other scenes of fondness, sensual looks and deportment, were presented before me, which sent a thrill of horror through my soul. Your arm encircled her waist, and the fondness expressed was having a bewitching influence. Then a curtain was lifted, and I was shown you in bed with ______. My Guide said, 'Iniquity, adultery' " (letter 16, 1888).

Evidently the second letter was enough to convince the man that his affair had been discovered, for at a private meeting the parties involved made "humble confessions" (letter 27, 1888).

In the early 1870s Ellen White once walked into a camp meeting tent service and interrupted the speaker, whom she had never met before, publicly accusing him of leading a double life and practicing polygamy. As the speaker fled, his brother, who was sitting in the audience, confirmed that the charge was true. A revival broke out at that camp meeting (for documentation and similar material, see Roger Coon, *Gift of Light*, pp. 32-35).

It is important to keep in mind that by itself a valid prediction does not prove that a prophet is of God, for Satan has a limited ability to foretell the future, since his angels are silent observers of every human conversation and can also influence the course of events. Thus Deuteronomy 13:1-5 warns that if a prophet predicts the future correctly but begins to teach heresy, teaching the people to worship other gods, he is not from God. First John 4:1-6 gives the New Testament version of this test: a prophet must teach the truth about Christ. This brings us to the final and perhaps most important test of a prophet: harmony with previous revelation.

Harmony With Scripture—The teachings of any new prophet must agree with previous revelation. Paul wrote, "If anybody thinks he is a prophet or spiritually gifted, let him acknowledge that what I am writing to you is the Lord's command" (1 Cor. 14:37). The Holy Spirit will not contradict His own earlier teachings. Any true prophet must uphold Scripture as having infallible normative authority. Scripture is the final court of appeal.

Ellen White permeated her writings, all 25 million words of them, with Scripture. She maintained a subordinate role to the Bible, stating that her own writings are not an addition to Scripture but rather an unfolding of its principles, not to give new light, but made necessary because so many had departed from biblical teaching

(*Testimonies,* vol. 5, p. 665). She referred to herself as a "lesser light" whose purpose was to point to the "greater light" of Scripture (*Selected Messages,* book 3, p. 33). Once she wrote, "If the *Testimonies* speak not according to the Word of God, reject them" (*Testimonies,* vol. 5, p. 691). In fact, in 1901 she even went so far as to tell some of her followers to stop quoting her writings until they were prepared to obey the Bible's teachings (*Selected Messages,* book 3, p. 33).

Thus Ellen White believed in the doctrine of sola scriptura, properly understood. "The Bible, and the Bible alone," she wrote, "is our rule of faith," as opposed to "the sayings and doings of men" (*Counsels on Sabbath School Work,* p. 84). "The words of the Bible, and the Bible alone, should be heard from the pulpit," as opposed to "tradition and human theories and maxims" (*Prophets and Kings,* p. 626). "The Bible, and the Bible alone, is to be our creed, the sole bond of union" in contrast to "our own views and ideas" (*Selected Messages,* book 1, p. 416). "The Bible, and the Bible only, is the religion of Protestants," as opposed to "the authority of tradition" (*The Great Controversy,* p. 448). We should "maintain the Bible, and the Bible only, as the standard of all doctrines and the basis of all reforms," as opposed to "the opinions of learned men, the deductions of science, [and] the creeds or decisions of ecclesiastical councils"(*ibid.,* p. 595). Tradition can never set aside inspiration (Matt. 15:3-9)

Although she upheld the Bible as the ultimate standard of doctrine, Ellen White did not hesitate to claim normative authority for her writings. "I am thankful," she wrote in 1906, "that the instruction contained in my books establishes present truth for this time. These books were written under the demonstration of the Holy Spirit" (letter 50, 1906). Scripture teaches that both apostles *and prophets* constitute the foundation of the church (Eph. 2:20) and receive authoritative revelations of new light not revealed to previous generations (Eph. 3:5).

Later revelation must not contradict earlier, but it may bring to the surface principles that may be only obscurely implicit in the earlier writings. A true prophet does not merely repeat the old truths, but brings forth things both old and new from the treasury of truth (Matt. 13:52). In the Bible there is room for both restoration and innovation. Accepting only the old wine in the old bottles leaves no room for new revelation.

Paul claimed that his teachings completely harmonized with the Jewish canon, the Old Testament: "I believe everything that agrees with the Law and that is written in the Prophets" (Acts 24:14); "I am saying nothing beyond what the prophets and Moses said would happen" (Acts 26:22). In the same way Ellen G. White said that her writings faithfully reflected the Christian canon, the Bible. Yet Paul's writings do say some things that the Old Testament does not explicitly bring out. Where there is continuity, we also find innovation. Because of this, the traditional Jews of Paul's day denied that his teachings were scriptural. " 'This man,' they charged, 'is persuading the people to worship God in ways contrary to the law' " (Acts 18:13). Paul was saying some things in a new way. So traditional Christians often reject Ellen White because she does not agree with their theological tradition, especially when their tradition is not scriptural.

Whenever the gift of prophecy is revived in the church, God brings some new understanding of truth to His people that may sound strange to those who have grown comfortable with the ecclesiastical status quo. Ellen White wrote:

"In every age there is a new development of truth, a message of God to the people of that generation. The old truths are all essential; new truth is not independent of the old, but an unfolding of it. It is only as the old truths are understood that we can comprehend the new. When

Christ desired to open to His disciples the truth of His resurrection, He began 'at Moses and all the prophets' and 'expounded unto them in all the scriptures the things concerning himself.' (Luke 24:47). But it is the light which shines in the fresh unfolding of truth that glorifies the old. He who rejects or neglects the new does not really possess the old. For him it loses its vital power and becomes but a lifeless form" (*Christ's Object Lessons,* pp. 127, 128).

One writer has compared the writings of Ellen White to a telescope focused on the sky of scriptural truth. The telescope does not put any new stars in the sky, but when you look through the telescope, you can see stars that are not visible to the naked eye. The telescope is necessary only because of our weak eyesight.

Like all the other tests, the test of conformity to Scripture is not sufficient by itself to establish anyone as a prophet, for even an uninspired person may teach truth. But a true prophet will turn men back to the Scriptures. And Ellen White certainly did.

In 1909 she gave her last public sermon. As she closed, she began to walk away from the pulpit; then, suddenly she turned, picked up her Bible, and held it up before the people, saying, "Brethren and sisters, I commend unto you this Book." Then she sat down. The last public statement she ever uttered was to exalt the Word of God.

Six years later she fell and broke her hip, from which she never recovered. In 1915 Ellen White died as she had lived: quoting Scripture. Her last words were "I know in whom I have believed."

The restoration of prophecy is one of God's greatest gifts to His remnant church. His people have received great blessings whenever they have followed the counsel of His messenger. But why don't you find out for yourself? The writings of Ellen White, like the Bible, are self-authenticating. Occasionally after reading one of her books for the first time, someone unfamiliar with the author will exclaim, "This woman was inspired!" It is not enough to read about them—you must read them for yourself. Try it and see.

Chapter 7

Inspiration: Words, Thoughts, or "Impressions"?

The fascinating study of how inspiration works is foundational to all else. Many controversies in other areas of theology stem from an imperfect understanding of the nature of inspiration. Chapters 7 through 9 will deal with this important topic.

As for approaches to a theory of inspiration, today we find two extremes—two ditches on either side of the highway of truth—that we must avoid simply because the facts contradict them.

On the one hand is encounter theology. Though the average person may not meet this theory directly, its pervasive influence demands that he or she have some knowledge of it. Encounter theology states that inspiration does not involve the transmission of objective facts or propositions. An encounter with God does not impart any real knowledge. Instead, the prophet has a subjective mystical experience that he interprets and records in ways that conform to his culture and his preconceived opinions. Those scholars who hold this theory—and they are many—stress the importance of such a life-transforming experience with God. Scripture seeks to reproduce such an encounter in the life of each believer, not to pass on doctrinal information.

It is true, of course, that Scripture's ultimate purpose is to bring the believer to an encounter with God, but this does not exhaust its function. Scripture is not merely a witness to God's previous meetings with men; it is God's Word and contains propositional truth that He communicated to His prophets.

An interesting story in 2 Kings 6 illustrates the objective, informational nature of revelation. Back in the days of the prophet Elisha, the king of Aram was at war with Israel; here and there he set up ambushes for the Israelites, but somehow they always managed to avoid them. Soon it became obvious that the king had an intelligence leak somewhere. When the ruler interrogated his officers, they told him that "Elisha, the prophet who is in Israel, tells the king of Israel the very words you speak in your bedroom" (verse 12). The Lord continued to reveal to Elisha the position of the Arameans and eventually delivered them into Israel's hand. Obviously, Elisha was receiving actual information from God.

Encounter theology rests upon certain naturalistic presuppositions. That is, it is based upon the assumption that genuine miracles are impossible. People often take such a position because neither they nor their friends have ever experienced one. But this is no more logical than the assumption that China does not exist because neither I nor my friends have ever been there. The reality of miracles has ample documentation for those who care to look. To start with an automatic rejection of the supernatural is to begin with a closed mind, not an open one.

It is clear from our study of fulfilled prophecy and other supernatural phenomena in the last two chapters that the prophet's message is more than the subjective record of a mystical contact with God. Encounter theology robs the Bible of any authority for us today. It appeals to those who would prefer to ignore those commands and predictions of Scripture that they find inconvenient.

Even those churches that do not endorse encounter theology can fall into the same ditch by setting aside unpopular scriptural mandates by saying that they are culturally conditioned and not relevant to us today. Many denominations whose sophisticated casuistry enables them to sidestep the hard sayings of Scripture end up by negating its absolute authority. The end result is often an emasculated gospel and a bankrupt theology. Such churches, unwilling to offend by confronting sin and popular error, often lose members in droves, for they have little to offer. We must guard well against such a temptation.

We have seen that it is not correct to say that the prophet receives only vague "impressions" from his experience with God. But if encounter theology is the ditch on the left-hand shoulder of the highway of truth, then verbal inspiration is the danger on the right-hand side. This theory of inspiration has great popularity among conservative groups today. It holds that God dictated the very words of the Bible to His prophets, who wrote them down exactly as they received them, without exercising any creative choice in the language.

The theory's supporters often cite texts that contain the term *word* with the implication that God gave the very words of the prophet's message. However, *word* in Scripture generally means "message." "The word of the Lord" indicates God's message, not the specific words.

It is no doubt true that some statements are verbally inspired, such as the Ten Commandments, written with God's own finger; or the words of an angel, spoken in vision and put in quotation marks by Ellen White. However, we find some very serious problems with the theory that all prophetic writing is verbally inspired.

The four Gospel accounts provide a definitive test of the theory of verbal inspiration, for just as the Bible writers record the words of God, so do the four different writers chronicle the words of Christ. If the theory of verbal inspiration is true—if the exact words are critical—then we would expect the different writers to use exactly the same phrases when reporting the same saying of Christ. It is one thing for writers to differ in their description of the same event, but surely a direct quotation from the mouth of the Lord would require verbatim reproduction.

But even a cursory examination of the Gospels will reveal that they vary, sometimes drastically, in reporting what Jesus said. In fact, it is almost impossible to find a single story or discourse in which the Lord's words are identical in each Gospel.

Consider the parable of the talents (Matt. 25:14-30; Luke 19:11-27). In Matthew the king gives five talents to one servant, two to another, and one to a third; whereas in Luke the nobleman presents all 10 servants the same amount of money: one mina. Matthew has each of the first two servants doubling his money and each receives the same reward. However, Luke has the first servant turning his mina into 10 and receiving 10 cities to rule, while the second transforms his mina into 5 and the king bestows 5 cities for him to govern. In addition, we observe verbal differences in every line.

Here is another example: according to Matthew 26:55, Jesus said to the Pharisees, "You did not arrest me." Mark 14:49 renders His words as "You did not arrest me." But Luke 22:53 has Him saying, "You did not lay a hand on me." If one report is verbally accurate, then the others are not. Yet the thought is the same in all three cases.

In Mark 9:43 Jesus states, "If your hand causes you to sin, cut it off." But Matthew 18:8 adds something: "If your hand or your foot causes you to sin, cut it off and throw it away."

We could cite hundreds of such examples. You may find them by opening to any passage in the Gospels at random and checking the parallel references in the other three Gospels. Much of the time the exact words are not so important—it's the thought that counts.

Ellen White, who herself was inspired, explained that inspiration provides thoughts, not words: "The Bible is not given to us in grand, superhuman language. Jesus, in order to reach man where he is, took humanity. The Bible must be given in the language of men. Everything that is human is imperfect. Different meanings are expressed by the same word; there is not one word for each distinct idea. The Bible was given for practical purposes. . . .

"The Bible is written by inspired men, but it is not God's mode of thought and expression. It is that of humanity. God, as a writer, is not represented. Men will often say such an expression is not like God. But God has not put Himself in words, in logic, in rhetoric, on trial in the Bible. The writers of the Bible were God's penmen, not His pen. Look at the different writers.

"It is not the words of the Bible that are inspired, but the men that were inspired. Inspiration acts not on the man's words or his expressions but on the man himself, who, under the influence of the Holy Ghost, is imbued with thoughts. But the words receive the impress of the individual mind. The divine mind is diffused. The divine mind and will is combined with the human mind and will; thus the utterances of the man are the word of God" (manuscript 24, 1886; in *Selected Messages*, book 1, pp. 20, 21).

One argument against verbal inspiration comes from the thousands of variant readings in the extant Hebrew and Greek manuscripts of the Bible. Such differences arose over the course of centuries as one scribe after another copied the manuscript. The vast majority of them are trivial, of the jot and tittle variety. Rarely is the meaning significantly affected. But if God dictated the Bible to the prophets verbatim, then why did He allow the copyists' errors to undo such perfection when He might easily have prevented it? If it was necessary to preserve the exact words of God, then why did He not protect them? Infallible dictation is worthless without infallible transmission.

Furthermore, infallible dictation has no value without infallible translation. Some biblical words have no exact counterpart in another language, and any given verse may have several possible translations. If only the exact Hebrew and Greek words are the correct words of God, then no translation can be the word of God. But if it is the meaning that is inspired, then translation is not a problem, for translation can convey meaning. On the other hand, if it is the exact words that are inspired, then no English translation of the Bible can claim inspiration.

Let us examine still another compelling argument against verbal inspiration. If the Bible were verbally inspired, we would expect to find flawless diction and uniformity of literary style throughout. But that is not the case. We observe wide variation in style and vocabulary among the different writers. Some writers of the New Testament use polished Greek, and others employ poor Greek. If God dictated the very words, we would not expect the ungrammatical language that we find in several New Testament books, such as Revelation.

The only theory that can account for all of this is thought inspiration. God does not give words to the prophet, but ideas, and the prophet puts the ideas in his own words.

"The Creator of all ideas may impress different minds with the same thought, but each may express it in a different way, yet without contradiction. The fact that this difference exists should not perplex or confuse us. It is seldom that two persons will view and express truth in the very same way. Each dwells on particular points which his constitution and education have fitted him to appreciate" (letter 53, 1900; in *Selected Messages*, book 1, p. 22).

The Use of Secretaries—Since inspired authors are not always polished writers, they sometimes need help to correct their faulty grammar and spelling. In ancient times it was a common practice for a public figure unskilled at composition to employ a secretary to write for him. Several scriptural authors followed this practice. A study of how they used the services of a secretary will shed some light on how inspiration works.

In Bible times such secretaries were known as amanuenses. Sometimes the amanuensis merely took dictation verbatim. But other times the author entrusted him with determining the final wording of the letter, often allowing a great deal of leeway. The professional writer took down the substance of the author's thoughts in shorthand and later (at his leisure, since transcribing was a laborious business) would write up the letter. The completed letter he then presented to the author for final approval and signature.

Paul used secretaries rather extensively. We have evidence that he allowed them some degree of freedom in choosing their own words and phrases to describe his ideas, because different sets of letters written by different secretaries have varying styles and vocabularies. For example, the Pastoral Epistles (Timothy and Titus) have a different style and vocabulary than Romans. So different, in fact, that today many critical scholars deny that the same person could have written both. But the solution to this problem is not to deny Pauline authorship but to recognize that he employed different ghostwriters with the various books. Paul provided the ideas but allowed his secretaries to phrase them.

Sometimes the secretary added a little note of his own, such as we find in Romans 16:22, where Paul's assistant writes, "I, Tertius, who wrote down this letter, greet you in the Lord." The apostle usually added a few words in his own handwriting near the end of each letter, as we find in Galatians 6:11, Colossians 4:18, and 1 Corinthians 16:21. Indeed, he states in 2 Thessalonians 3:17 that he always does so as a way to show that the letter is authentic. Sometimes, of course, Paul had no secretary available and had to write the entire letter by himself (note Philemon 19).

Peter's secretary, named Silvanus or Silas (1 Peter 5:12), was a man of some literary accomplishment who apparently coauthored the Thessalonian Epistles (1 Thess. 1:1; note the use of "we" throughout the letters). Not only does this account for the extensive verbal parallels between 1 Peter and 1 and 2 Thessalonians, but it may also explain the excellent Greek of 1 Peter as compared with the rough Greek in the Second Epistle.

We can observe a similar difference between the excellent Greek of the Gospel of John and the very defective Greek of Revelation, probably resulting from the fact that John had no secretary during his exile on the Isle of Patmos. Such a situation would explain, for example, why the word *Jerusalem* is consistently spelled one way in John and another way in Revelation. Evidently inspiration does not provide correct grammar and spelling.

The use of a secretary is not without risk, as far as the prophet's credibility is concerned. Jeremiah's secretary was Baruch (Jer. 36:4), and although he seems to have served only as a stenographer, taking dictation, the prophet's critics accused him of being influenced by his secretary. "But Baruch son of Neriah is inciting you against us to hand us over to the Babylonians, so they may kill us or carry us into exile to Babylon" (Jer. 43:3).

Ellen White's Secretaries—Ellen White also used a number of secretaries to assist her in her writing. Like John the revelator's, Ellen White's grammar was not very polished, and she needed the help of others to correct it. She felt keenly her shortcomings as a writer. She was afraid that her words would fall short of the glory of the subjects she was treating:

"I walk with trembling before God. I know not how to speak or trace with pen the large subject of the atoning sacrifice. I know not how to present subjects in the living power in which they stand before me. I tremble for fear lest I shall belittle the great plan of salvation by cheap words. I bow my soul in awe and reverence before God and say, 'Who is sufficient for these things?' " (letter 40, 1892).

"That which is holy and elevated in heavenly things, I scarcely dare represent. Often I lay down my pen and say, Impossible, impossible for finite minds to grasp eternal truths, and deep holy principles, and to express their living import. I stand ignorant and helpless. The rich current of thought takes possession of my whole being, and I lay down my pen, and say, O Lord, I am finite, I am weak, and simple and ignorant; Thy grand and holy revelations I can never find language to express" (manuscript 23, 1896).

At first her husband was her editor. "The instruction I received in vision was faithfully written out by me, as I had time and strength for the work. Afterward we examined the matter together, my husband correcting grammatical errors and eliminating needless repetition" (*Selected Messages,* book 1, p. 50). But after suffering a stroke, he could no longer help her, and she bemoaned her inability to write fluently. "I am not a scholar. I cannot prepare my own writings for the press. . . . I am not a grammarian" (manuscript 3, 1873). Once she asked J. H. Waggoner, a minister with literary talent, to examine a manuscript, hoping that "if there is any wording of doctrinal points not so clear as might be, he might discern it" (letter 4a, 1876). When she received the manuscript back with virtually no changes, she was disappointed. "I put copy in Elder Waggoner's hand to copy," she wrote.

"He just did a miserable job. He did not change anything or improve it at all" (letter 59, 1876). In time she came to rely largely on hired secretaries to do the job, though others also played a part:

"I have all my publications closely examined. I desire that nothing shall appear in print without careful investigation. Of course I would not want men who have not a Christian experience, or are lacking in ability to appreciate literary merit, to be placed as judges of what is essential to come before the people, as pure provender thoroughly winnowed from the chaff. I laid out all my manuscript on *Patriarchs and Prophets* and on Volume IV [*The Great Controversy*] before the book committee for examination and criticism. I also placed these manuscripts in the hands of some of our ministers for examination. The more criticism of them the better for the work" (letter 49, 1894).

Keep in mind that it was not the thought but the wording that she wanted criticized. No one was "permitted to add matter or change the meaning" (*Selected Messages,* book 1, p. 50) of Ellen White's messages. Her son, who was intimately connected with her editorial activities, explains:

"The secretaries and copyists who prepare Mother's writings for the printer remove repetitions so that the matter may be brought into the allotted space. They correct bad grammar and they fit the matter for publication. They sometimes carry her best expressions of thought from one paragraph to another but do not introduce their own thoughts into the matter. The thoughts and the expressions which you mention are Mother's own thoughts and expressions" (W. C. White to Julia Malcolm, Dec. 10, 1894).

Ellen White had the final say-so. She read and approved all changes to make sure that the wording correctly represented the will of the Holy Spirit. Thus the final phrasing was her own either by creation or adoption: "I read over all that is copied, to see that everything is as it should be. I read all the book manuscript before it is sent to the printer" (letter 133, 1902). God guided so that the final result was the product of inspiration.

The only way to find out how inspiration works is to examine its product, for nowhere does Scripture give an explicit, detailed account of how inspiration functions. The evidence indicates that we must reject liberal theories that deny the possibility of objective revelation. God imparts to the prophet not merely emotional impressions but actual facts. On the other hand, we must also spurn fundamentalist "straitjacket" theories that allow an author no individuality in the production of an inspired document. The prophet receives neither exact words nor vague impressions, but definite ideas.

Chapter 8

Inerrancy: Where the Battle Isn't

Many good Christians have been taught that the Bible is *inerrant,* or free from any sort of contradiction or inaccuracy in the modern scientific sense. The concept of inerrancy has become a shibboleth of religious fundamentalists, and rhetorical battles continue to rage over the doctrine.

Those who believe in inerrancy reason something like this:

God does not err.

The Bible is the Word of God.

Therefore, the Bible cannot err.

But is that a valid argument? Let's compare a similar syllogism:

God does not need sleep.

Jesus was God.

Therefore, Jesus did not need sleep.

Obviously something is wrong with our second syllogism, for Jesus apparently did sleep (Mark 4:38). The fallacy in both arguments lies in the minor premise, on the second line: Jesus was not merely the Son of God, but was also the Son of man. Likewise, the Bible is not simply the Word of God, written by God's finger and dropped from heaven. It is also the words of man. "The Bible, with its God-given truths expressed in the language of men," writes Ellen White, "presents a union of the divine and the human" (*Selected Messages*, book 1, p. 25). However, that does not mean that it is partly divine and partly human. Rather, like Christ, it is fully divine and fully human.

Those who insist on inerrancy fail to recognize the dual divine/human nature of Scripture. The position of inerrancy resembles the ancient error of Docetism in Christology. The Docetists denied the humanity of our Lord, claiming that Christ only *seemed* to be human. Likewise, modern fundamentalists reject the humanity of the Bible.

Such an untenable position will eventually lead an enlightened inquirer to lose faith in the Bible because of problems that such a rigid concept of inspiration can never account for. The Pharisees rejected Christ because He did not measure up to their preconceived ideas about His role. They were looking not only for a military champion but an impeccable messiah. But this Man dined with sinners, was lax in His Sabbath observance, and ate with unwashed hands—not very messiah-like behavior, from their viewpoint. Modern expectations of an impeccable Bible will meet with similar disappointment. Just as Christ did not always act as a perfect Jew might be expected to act, so the Bible might not conform to our ideas of historical, scientific, or grammatical perfection.

Many of the great thinkers of the Christian church, such as Augustine, Luther, and Wesley, have maintained that there are no errors, no matter how slight, in Scripture. Wesley went so far as to propose the rule "false in one, false in all," maintaining that a single error would discredit the Bible as the Word of God. With such a prestigious pedigree, it is no wonder that many Christians use the same argument today. If we cannot believe everything, they say, we cannot believe anything.

The concept sounds reasonable at first, but it is not. When I was in high school, my algebra text had a section in the back of the book that listed the answers to the homework problems in the front. Occasionally the class discovered an error in one of these answers, but that did not cause anyone to lose confidence in the theorems presented in the front of the book. While the text contained a few minor numerical errors, it did not teach error. The basic principles it contained were valid and true.

Scripture itself indicates that the gift of prophecy has limitations. First Corinthians 13:8-12 refers to the knowledge that comes through inspired revelation as being partial and imperfect, falling far short of the complete knowledge that we will have in the perfection of the new age. Knowing and prophesying only in part, we see through a glass darkly—but we do see. God mediates His perfect wisdom through an imperfect vehicle. "We have this treasure in jars of clay" (2 Cor. 4:7). The divine message of the Bible is perfect, but it is in "jars of clay," which are imperfect.

It is a common misconception that prophets have continuous insight into all theological questions and that they have supernatural knowledge of any situation in which they find themselves. But unless the prophet receives a special revelation, his knowledge is limited to his natural senses. According to 2 Kings 4:27, God sometimes hides things from His prophets. Although an inspired writer of Scripture, David apparently believed Ziba's lie about Mephibosheth and acted on the basis of his false information (2 Sam. 16:1-4; 19:24-30). Thus prophets sometimes make mistakes. "No man that lives is infallible," writes Ellen White (*Review and Herald*, Mar. 25, 1890). She says of the apostles in Jerusalem that "though some of these men wrote under the inspiration of the Spirit of God, yet when not under its direct influence they sometimes erred" (*Sketches From the Life of Paul*, p. 214).

Second Samuel 7 tells of a prophet giving erroneous advice. King David called in Nathan to ask his reaction to

David's plan to build a temple in which to house the ark of the testimony. Nathan gave his approval, saying, "Whatever you have in mind, go ahead and do it, for the Lord is with you." However, that night God spoke to the prophet and told him to go back and tell David that it was not he, but his son, who should build a house for the Lord. A vision quickly corrected Nathan's wrong advice.

Something similar happened to Paul on his prison voyage. He warned his captors that the journey would end in great loss of both cargo and lives (Acts 27:10). However, a vision soon prompted him to alter his prediction: Nobody would perish on the ship (Acts 27:22).

In 1902 a committee of men led by A. G. Daniells persuaded Ellen White to give her verbal approval to a plan to close down the recently opened Southern Publishing Association in Nashville because it was losing $1,000 per month. But that evening Mrs. White had a vision that reversed her stand, and she wrote Daniells immediately. Several weeks later she commented, "During the night following our interview in my house and out on the lawn under the trees, October 19, 1902, in regard to the work in the Southern field, the Lord instructed me that I had taken a wrong position" (letter 208, 1902).

In all of the cases mentioned so far, the problem merely involved the prophet's verbal counsel, and a vision quickly corrected the mistake. However, even when writing under inspiration, a prophet may suffer a lapse of memory. In 1 Corinthians 1:14-16 Paul writes, "I am thankful that I did not baptize any of you except Crispus and Gaius, so no one can say that you were baptized into my name. (Yes, I also baptized the household of Stephanas; beyond that, I don't remember if I baptized anyone else.)" Here Paul makes a misstatement, modifies it, then confesses that he simply cannot remember who he has baptized.

Sometimes inspired writers forgot who wrote what in the Old Testament. Matthew 27:9, 10 attributes a quotation from Zechariah to Jeremiah, and Mark 1:2 ascribes a quote from Malachi to Isaiah. In 1913 Ellen White wrote, "The love of Christ constraineth us, the apostle Peter declared," though it was actually Paul who said it (2 Cor. 5:14).

We find scores of such minor discrepancies in Scripture. For example: did David kill 40,000 horsemen (2 Sam. 10:18), or footmen (1 Chron. 19:18)? Did the cock crow once when Peter denied the Lord (Matt. 26:34, 69-75), or twice (Mark 14:66-72)? Does Cainan (Luke 3:36) belong between Salah and Arphaxad, or not (Gen. 11:12)? Did 24,000 die in the plague (Num. 25:9), or 23,000 (1 Cor. 10:8)? Did Solomon have 40,000 stalls for his horses (1 Kings 4:26), or 4,000 (2 Chron. 9:25)? Was Jehoachin 18 when he began to reign (2 Kings 24:8) or 8 (2 Chron. 36:9)? Did Ahaziah come to the throne at the age of 22 (2 Kings 8:26), or 42 (2 Chron. 22:2)? Why does the description of the dedication of the covenant in Hebrews 9:19-21 differ so much from that given by Moses in Exodus 24:5-8? Was Goliath killed by David (1 Sam. 17), or Elhanan (2 Sam. 21:19)? Will lions inhabit the new earth (Isa. 11:6, 7; 65:25), or not (Isa. 35:9)? Did Jesus drink the painkilling potion offered to Him on the cross (John 19:28-30), or not (Matt. 27:34)? Was He crucified at the third hour (Mark 15:25), or several hours later (John 19:14)? Did Christ allow His disciples to carry a staff (Mark 6:8), or forbid them (Matt. 10:9, 10)? Did the centurion send friends to tell Christ that he was not worthy to have Him come under his roof (Luke 7:6), or did he go himself (Matt. 8:5-13)? Was it James and John who asked for special favors (Mark 10:35ff.), or their mother (Matt. 20:20ff.)? We could make a similar list of discrepancies in the writings of Ellen White.

Those who believe in biblical inerrancy go to extreme lengths to explain such problems away. They put forth rather farfetched arguments to harmonize the differences. As a last resort, they argue that the errors did not appear in the original manuscript (the *autograph*), but crept in as the manuscripts were copied and recopied by hand over the course of the centuries. It was not the original author but a later scribe who originated the mistake.

Unfortunately, the evidence does not support such a theory. Whenever a copyist has introduced an error into the text, we usually find some sort of manuscript evidence at that point—some will preserve the correct reading, while others retain the error. But when all extant manuscripts read exactly the same—as they do in most of the problematic passages listed above—there is little chance that we are dealing with a copyist's error. Furthermore, it is a well-known axiom in the science of textual criticism that when the pious scribes changed the text, they did so not to introduce a discrepancy but to solve one. If they altered their text, it was to bring it into harmony with a parallel passage, not to create a contradiction.

It is better to be honest with the evidence than to attempt to solve such problems by tortuous sophistry. The difficulties we have been examining are mostly trivial. In no way do they affect our doctrine or our behavior, and evidently God did not think them vital enough to correct. But it is important that we be aware of them so that we do not take extreme positions about the inspiration of Scripture only to face disillusionment in the end. Let us not set the front lines of the battle so far forward that, once dug in, we find ourselves forced to retreat. Defenders of inerrancy are fighting the wrong battle.

Minor discrepancies in Scripture do not affect the basic teachings. Though there is static on the communications channel, the message comes through clearly. The static does not alter the concepts. We have seen that whenever a prophet makes a significant mistake, the Lord corrects him. God does not allow any serious error that would affect the Bible's basic reliability. Thus the Bible is, in fact, an infallible guide in matters of faith and morals.

By faith and morals, we are simply saying that we should not use the Bible in ways contrary to its intentions. The Bible is not a textbook on mathematics, and it is foolish to try to derive the value of pi (3.1416, the ratio of the circumference of a circle to its diameter) from the measurements of the Temple basin given in 1 Kings 7:23, as some scholars eager to find things to criticize in the Bible have done. We should not claim more for the Bible than it does for itself. The Bible is not a scientific handbook, and we must not interpret statements intended to teach piety as if they were scientific facts.

For example, Jesus said that the mustard seed was the smallest of seeds (Mark 4:31). Now it is a fact that various seeds of the orchid family are even tinier than mustard seeds, but Jesus was not giving a lecture on botany, rather making a point about faith, using a hyperbolic expression not meant to be taken literally.

Likewise, Psalm 93:1 and 96:10 say that the earth shall not be moved, and theologians in the Middle Ages used these passages as proof texts against Galileo's theory that the earth travels through space. Of course, the psalmist was not talking about physical movement (cf. Ps. 15:5, KJV, which says that the righteous man will "never be moved"). To base our cosmology on such statements is wrong.

Does this mean that Scripture is scientifically unreliable? No. The Bible *does* contain material far in advance of its contemporary culture. Some of the Mosaic laws on diet and hygiene, for example, are so far ahead of their time that we can only explain them as products of inspiration.

Genesis 17 specifies the circumcisions of newborn children on the eighth day. Today we know that the clotting factor (prothrombin) in an infant's blood is deficient until then, at which time it rises to above normal levels, so that not until that point will a child be able to sustain injury without excessive bleeding. How would an ancient writer, even one "educated in all the wisdom of the Egyptians" (Acts 7:22), have known that fact, especially since most surrounding cultures did not perform circumcision until the teenage years? Keep in mind that we possess an ancient Egyptian medical text contemporary with Moses, the Ebers papyrus. It is full of ridiculous remedies for disease that include such ingredients as lizard blood, swine's teeth, putrid meat, stinking fat, moisture from pigs' ears, milk, goose grease, asses' hooves, and excreta from various animals. Contrast that with the laws of cleanliness in the books of Leviticus and Numbers. The ravage of the Black Death in the fourteenth century was finally halted only when clerics applied the laws of Leviticus 13, which applied to sanitation and isolation of the infected. (See S. I. McMillen, *None of These Diseases*, chaps. 1, 2.)

It seems that whenever the Bible deals with things that have to do with our physical or spiritual well-being, or when an important point of faith is involved (such as in the Creation account), it speaks with scientific accuracy.

A good example is the story of Jacob's experience as a shepherd, found in Genesis 30. Jacob, who has been herding Laban's flocks, asks that he might keep all the speckled and spotted lambs as pay for his labor. They would be easy to distinguish from the white sheep belonging to Laban. In order to increase his flock, Jacob took some branches and peeled the bark off in strips to make them speckled and spotted, and then placed them in front of the watering troughs where the stronger females in heat could clearly see them. He believed that such a practice would cause their offspring to be speckled and spotted. Critics have wrongly ridiculed his superstition as an example of error in the Bible. Had they but read further, they would have found that the passage contains a remarkably advanced understanding of genetics, for the following chapter (Gen. 31:10-12) describes a dream in which God showed Jacob that the increased production of speckled and spotted lambs did not result from his scheming but from the fact that the females had mated with male goats that carried the traits for speckling and spotting. It was important to correct Jacob's mistaken scientific notions in this case because he assumed that he was the architect of his own prosperity, and was taking credit due God alone. The glory of God was at stake. Not until Gregor Mendel came along in the nineteenth century did we understand the genetic principles implied in this passage.

Thus we have clear evidence that God granted His prophets supernatural insight into matters that affected them in some practical way. However, we should not always expect to find advanced scientific concepts in the Bible in cases where no important theological point is at stake, for God can only teach His children so much at one time. First of all, He must correct their theological and ethical errors. It is not important that they understand such things as the fact that stars are distant suns. And the more strange ideas God put in His Word, the harder it would be for His people to accept it. If men had to adopt Einstein's theory of relativity as a part of Christianity, how many would be Christians?

Thus we should not be surprised if the Bible seems to reflect the cosmological or even astrological views of its culture (e.g., "From the heavens the stars fought, from their courses they fought against Sisera" [Judges 5:20]). God may allow an inspired writer to use the language of a commonly held pseudoscientific belief if it has no ethical or theological relevance, since correcting it would impose just one more unnecessary ideological barrier between prophet and people, making it difficult to correct more essential errors. For example, people in New Testament times believed that the heart was the seat of reason and the bowels the center of the emotions. We see the belief reflected in contemporary technical lists of the anatomical functions of the body (2 Enoch 65:2; Testament of Naphtali 2:7, 8). Clearly this was not just a figure of speech, and evidently God did not feel that it was important enough to correct at that time.

God gave us the Bible for practical purposes. Ellen White writes: "Christ imparted only that knowledge which could be utilized. His instruction of the people was confined to the needs of their own condition in practical life" (*Testimonies*, vol. 8, p. 310). Scripture does not seek to reveal to us advanced scientific truths, or to make us financially rich, or even to answer all of our questions about God. But it *is* "useful for . . . training in righteousness" (2 Tim. 3:16). It does promise that it will leave us "wise for salvation" (verse 15)—which eventually brings all other blessings in its train.

Even in the area of its proper domain—theology—Scripture contains things difficult to understand. But we should expect this of a book authored by the Supreme Intelligence in the universe. Although we find an amazing unity in its teachings, that unity is not uniformity. Inspiration does not force all prophets into the same theological mold, but allows for differences of viewpoint. Its paradoxes are an essential mark of the transcendent, which cannot be fully comprehended by any one person—not even a prophet.

For example, Paul and James come to apparently differing conclusions on the question of the grounds of justification (cf. Rom. 3; James 2). James says we are justified by faith and works, while Paul argues for faith without works. Paul evidently felt that the greatest danger to the church was legalism, while James saw a powerful threat from libertinism. I believe it is safe to say that each writer was somewhat uncomfortable with the theology of the other, for we have other evidence in the New Testament that the two writers did not see eye-to-eye.

Although James basically supported Paul's position at the Jerusalem Council of Acts 15, Paul was evidently not in total agreement with the ceremonial stipulations retained by that council as a compromise, for he makes some rather broad exceptions to them in 1 Corinthians 8-10.

Some years later, when Paul last visited Jerusalem as a free man, we find evidence of tension between him and James in a conversation recorded in Acts 21:18-25. In verse 25 James reminds him that the agreement of Acts 15 applied only to the Gentile believers. James, as leader of the church, is gently rebuking Paul for allegedly teaching *Jewish* Christians that they are no longer bound by the stipulations of the ceremonial law (this is what Paul stands accused of teaching in verse 21). But the apostolic agreement of Acts 15 exempted only *Gentile* Christians from the law. It seems that the leaders of the church believed that the entire ceremonial law still applied to Jewish believers, and they saw Paul as the maverick who disagreed on the issue.

Paul's letter to the Galatians says nothing to allay their suspicions. Indeed, it provides further evidence for the rift by naming James as the one who originated the "circumcision group" that the apostle opposed (Gal. 2:12). Peter evidently sided with James. Notice his warning against libertinism in 2 Peter 2 and 3:17, and his statement that Paul's writings contain things hard to understand (2 Peter 3:16), which may be a polite way of saying that even he found them difficult to accept. Could this have had something to do with the falling out between the two that Paul described in Galatians 2:11-14?

Ellen White actually states that the apostles were at odds with some of Paul's innovative teachings: "Paul held to his inspired truth, and taught it to others, opposed as he was by the apostles, who ought to have upheld him.

. . . Paul's brethren withstood him. Those whom the Lord had used as His witnesses protested against him, and declared that he was advocating theories that were contrary to the fundamental principles which they had been taught. But Paul firmly held his ground" (*Review and Herald*, May 25, 1897).

Evidently the Holy Spirit saw that the church needed the viewpoints of both James and Paul, which, after all, are not really contradictory. Paul is talking about initial justification (forgiveness and acceptance), in which works play no part, while James is concentrating on ultimate justification in the judgment, at which time we will stand judged by our works—as even Paul teaches (Rom. 2:5-8; 2 Cor. 5:10). Furthermore, the "faith alone" of James is an empty assent, while Paul's "faith alone" is an active trust "that works by love" (Gal. 5:6).

Thus while Paul and James may have had varying approaches to the subject of salvation, they were not fundamentally different. In my candid examination of even the most difficult passages, I have uncovered nothing that indicates any real theological contradictions in Scripture. Whenever the viewpoints of the various writers appear on a surface level to be contradictory, it is an invitation to deeper study, which, in time, will reveal the underlying harmony.

The science of cartography (mapmaking) provides a useful analogy. It is impossible, even in theory, to map a sphere onto a plane (flat surface) without distortion. In other words, if we were to cut up a map of the earth in the form of an inflated rubber globe, we could not lay the pieces down flat on a table without stretching certain areas and hence altering the shape of the continents on them. So all flat maps contain distortions that are at their least in the center and greatest around the edges. For example, on some flat maps Greenland appears larger than North America, while on others it seems smaller. Now, Greenland cannot be both larger and smaller than the United States. But this apparent contradiction is an unavoidable result of transforming three-dimensional reality into two dimensions; both maps are correct according to their reference system. We can minimize this by using different maps for different purposes.

Our model may shed light on the nature of revelation. Somewhat the same problem exists when divine truth gets translated into human language. "The Bible, perfect as it is in its simplicity, does not answer to the great ideas of God; for infinite ideas cannot be perfectly embodied in finite vehicles of thought" (*Selected Messages,* book 1, p. 22). Truth is multidimensional, and no single perspective is sufficient. Furthermore, the whole of Scripture is greater than the sum of its parts. We may think of each Bible writer as a cartographer of divine truth. If taken alone, Paul's map of truth might produce a somewhat distorted picture of certain peripheral (to him) areas of truth—not because he makes false statements, but because he tends to emphasize certain themes and neglect others. However, James's map offsets this (and vice versa), for James takes up topics that lie on the fringes of Paul's map. Both maps, of course, are reliable when properly interpreted —which means as long as we concentrate on the main subject of the passage and do not seek to derive eternal verities from incidental allusions or points mentioned in passing. It would be a mistake to attempt a careful study of Antarctica from the fringes of a map of South America.

By analogy, any comprehensive theological atlas such as the Bible will contain paradoxes and antinomies. This is an essential mark of truth. Even the exact science of mathematics contains unresolvable paradoxes that continue to puzzle mathematicians. Any theological treatise that has no paradoxes must fall under the suspicion of triviality—an accusation that not even the Bible's worst critics have leveled against it.

In conclusion, although some scriptural passages may appear to clash with others on a surface level, a fundamental unity flows through the whole Book. Although the Bible is not impeccable, it is infallible. While we recognize the marks of humanity, we must never use them as an excuse to lessen its divine authority. The Inspired Writings are a reliable guide that, faithfully followed, will lead us home.

Chapter 9

A Prophet's Sources: Visions and More

God speaks to His prophets "in various ways" (Heb. 1:1). One of the most familiar ways is through visions. "When a prophet of the Lord is among you," God told Moses, "I reveal myself to him in visions, I speak to him in dreams" (Num. 12:6). However, sometimes God's prophets get their information in more mundane ways—by conversation with others (1 Cor. 1:11) or by reading (Dan. 9:2; Luke 1:1-4). Sometimes they incorporate something they have heard or read into their own writings. Some students of Scripture find this disturbing, feeling that if a prophet's information comes from God, he or she should not have to copy from other sources. Since this problem has been much discussed in recent times, we will examine it in some depth.

Over the past few centuries scholars have discovered hundreds of ancient texts, older than the Bible, that contain parallels to various passages of Scripture. It surprised some scholars to find such similarity and continuity where they expected only uniqueness and discontinuity, and so they jumped to unwarranted conclusions about the relationship between Scripture and such accounts.

For example, after archaeologists discovered the Gilgamesh Epic, a Babylonian account of the Creation and Flood, some assumed that the author of the Genesis account had derived his story from the earlier Babylonian source. Yet a careful examination of the evidence indicates otherwise. The Babylonian account, for example, says that the ark was shaped like a cube. Now a cube-shaped boat is terribly unseaworthy and would not last a day in a storm. But the dimensions of the ark given in Genesis 6:15 are those of an extremely seaworthy vessel, as evidenced by the success of modern vessels built with approximately the same dimensions. Evidently the Babylonian story is a corrupt version of an ancient event preserved more faithfully in Scripture. This sort of evidence invalidates theories that make Scripture dependent on pagan sources.

But although Scripture is in no sense based upon, or derived from, pagan sources, it sometimes borrows from them. The Song of Solomon uses phraseology drawn from the religious myths recited during the pagan new year's ceremony of ancient Sumer, a civilization that existed 3,000 years before Christ. Proverbs includes sayings from the wisdom literature of ancient Egypt and other Near Eastern cultures. Psalms employs wording found in Canaanite hymns to Baal. We find parallels between the laws of Moses and other ancient law codes, such as that of Hammurabi. What are we to make of this?

Nothing—we simply accept it. If God should inspire men to appropriate gems of truth or beauty previously used in the service of error and employ them for a holy purpose, more praise to His name. Such is the nature of redemption.

This phenomenon occurs as often in the New Testament as in the Old. Significant portions of the Gospels have parallels in other religious writings of the times. Rather than causing dismay, it is something that we should have expected. "The Light which has lightened every man from the beginning may shine more clearly but cannot change," wrote C. S. Lewis. "The Origin cannot suddenly start being, in the popular sense of the word, 'original' " (C. S. Lewis, *Reflections on the Psalms*, p. 27). Many cultures anticipated Him, because He anticipated them. After all, Christ was the Saviour not of the Jews only but of the whole world. Thus He not only fulfilled the prophecies of the Old Testament, but also many pagan myths and prophecies. The concept of virgin birth, of a great healer, and of supernatural darkness and earthquakes marking the death of a great king—things we find in the life of Christ—are better known in pagan than in Jewish circles. He did not leave Himself without witness in any nation.

Thus it is not surprising to find parallels between certain non-Jewish writings and the sayings of Christ. To cite just two examples: the Cynics' (those belonging to an ancient Greek school of philosophy) practice of possessing only a cloak, wallet, and staff reminds one of Mark 6:8: "Take nothing for the journey except a staff—no bread, no bag, no money in your belts." Part of Christ's sermon on the mount (Matt. 6:26-30) resembles a passage from a speech by Diogenes (Cynic founder, who died c. 320 B.C.), recorded in *Dio Chrysostom* 1:429: "Consider the beasts yonder and the birds, how much freer from trouble they live than men, and how much more happily also, how much healthier and stronger they are, and how each of them lives the longest life possible, although they have neither hands nor human intelligence. And yet, to counterbalance these and their limitations, they have one very great blessing—they own no property."

Although we observe many New Testament parallels to non-Jewish writings, the taproot of the New Testament is the literature of the Jews. This includes not only the Old Testament—the primary source—but also certain religious tracts composed during the period between the Testaments, 300 B.C. to A.D. 100, known today as the Apocrypha and pseudepigrapha. New Testament writers sometimes borrowed from such documents.

Christ's parable of the unproductive fig tree in Luke 13:6-9 resembles the following passage from Ahiqar 8:35 (Syriac), written some 600 years earlier: "My son, thou hast been to me like the palm tree that stood by a river, and cast all its fruit into the river; and when its lord came to cut it down, it said to him, 'Let me alone this year, and I will bring thee forth carobs.' "

The book of Sirach, found in the Apocrypha, was written around 180 B.C. The teachings of Christ echo various themes from it, such as the counsel that one should not offer repetitive prayers (Sir. 7:14), that one must forgive to be forgiven (Sir. 28:2), and that old wine is more desirable than new (Sir. 9:10). In Matthew 11:28-30 Christ said something that resembles a speech that Sirach put in the mouth of personified Wisdom: "Come unto me, ye unlearned, and lodge in my school. . . . Put your necks under her yoke, and let your souls receive instruction; it is to be found close by. See with your eyes that I have labored little, and found for myself much rest" (Sir. 51:23-27).

Sirach 11:18, 19, "There is a man who is rich through his diligence and self-denial, and this is the reward allotted to him: when he says, 'I have found rest, and now I shall enjoy my goods!' he does not know when his time will come; he will leave them to others and die," may have prompted Jesus' story of the rich fool with his barns (Luke 12:16-21).

We could multiply such examples from the Gospels many times over. Many parables of Christ are versions of contemporary stories found in Rabbinic Jewish writings, though Christ often gave them an original twist that sometimes infuriated His enemies.

Ellen White too employed secular sources. One of her comments on Christ's use of sources sheds light on her rationale:

"It was the work of Christ to present the truth in the framework of the gospel, and to reveal the precepts and principles that He had given to fallen mán. Every idea He presented was His own. He needed not to borrow thoughts from any, for He was the originator of all truth. *He could present the ideas of prophets and philosophers,* and preserve His originality; for all wisdom was His; He was the source, the fountain, of all truth" (*Selected Messages,* book 1, p. 409; italics supplied).

To an inspired writer, the ultimate source of all truths is God. The human source is irrelevant. The author of Ecclesiastes says something like this. Although Ecclesiastes includes ideas gleaned from contemporary wisdom literature, the writer says they came from God: "He pondered and searched out and set in order many proverbs. The Teacher searched to find just the right words, and what he wrote was upright and true. The words of the wise are like goads, their collected sayings like firmly embedded nails—given by one Shepherd" (Eccl. 12:9-11).

Ellen White too drew from many sources, including contemporary historians (used in writing *The Great Controversy),* devotional commentaries on Scripture (employed in composing *The Desire of Ages),* collections of sermons, books on prophecy, and various other works. Although she based the theological principles in her writings on visions and dreams, she was guided under inspiration in the selection of information from scores of other authors.

It is common for inspired historians to rely on secular histories for historical data. Old Testament historical books such as Samuel, Kings, and Chronicles seem to use information drawn from contemporary court annals and other histories like the original copy now which the author refers to by name (e.g., 1 Kings 11:41; 14:19, 29).

The Gospels themselves followed a somewhat similar pattern. Luke 1:1-4 indicates that the author did some research into the many accounts that others had already produced about Jesus, and then compiled his own chronological account on the basis of such sources. He mentions nothing about visions. As an author, he was an inspired researcher whose source of information was contemporary histories composed by other men.

However, prophetic borrowing extends beyond historical materials. It is equally common with theology and prophecy, as we see from the books of Revelation, Romans, and Hebrews. Numerous parallels exist between the book of Hebrews and the writings of the Jewish philosopher Philo (lived c. 50 B.C. to A.D. 25). Paul in Romans borrows ideas from the first century B.C. book of Wisdom, found in the Apocrypha:

Romans*	Wisdom†
Ever since the creation of the world his [God's] invisible nature, namely, his eternal power and deity, has been clearly perceived in the things that have been made. So they are without excuse; for although they knew God they did not honor him as God or give thanks to him, but they became futile in their thinking and their senseless minds were darkened. Claiming to be wise, they became fools, and exchanged the glory of the immortal God for images resembling mortal man or birds or animals or reptiles (1.20-23).	From the greatness and beauty of created things comes a corresponding perception of their Creator (13:5). Yet again, not even they are to be excused; for if they had the power to know so much that they could investigate the world, how did they fail to find sooner the Lord of these things? (13:8). For all men who were ignorant of God were foolish by nature; and they were unable from the good things that are seen to know him who exists, nor did they recognize the craftsman while paying heed to his works (13:1).
For this reason God gave	

them up to dishonorable passions. . . . They were filled with all manner of wickedness, evil, covetousness, malice. Full of envy, murder, strife, deceit, malignity, they are gossips, slanderers, haters of God, insolent, haughty, boastful, inventors of evil, disobedient to parents, foolish, faithless, heartless, ruthless (1:26-31).

Who are you, a man, to answer back to God? Will what is molded say to its molder, "Why have you made me thus?" Has the potter no right over the clay, to make out of the same lump one vessel for beauty and another for menial use? What if God, desiring to show his wrath and to make known his power, has endured with much patience the vessels of wrath made for destruction, in order to make known the riches of his glory for the vessels of mercy, which he has prepared beforehand for glory? (9:20-23).

———

*From the Revised Standard Version.

For they went far astray on the paths of error, accepting as gods those animals which even their enemies despised; they were deceived like foolish babes (12:24).

They no longer keep either their lives or their marriages pure, but they either treacherously kill one another, or grieve one another by adultery, and all is a raging riot of blood and murder, theft and deceit, corruption, faithlessness, tumult, perjury, confusion over what is good, forgetfulness of favors, pollution of souls, sex perversion, disorder in marriage, adultery, and debauchery (14:24-26).

For who will say [to God], "What hast thou done?" Or who will resist thy judgment? Who will accuse thee for the destruction of nations which thou didst make? (12:12).

For when a potter kneads the soft earth and laboriously molds each vessel for our service, he fashions out of the same clay both the vessels that serve clean uses and those for contrary uses, making all in like manner; but which shall be the use of each of these the worker in clay decides (15:7).

For if thou didst punish with such great care and indulgence the enemies of thy servants and those deserving of death, granting them time and opportunity to give up their wickedness, with what strictness thou hast judged thy sons! (12:20).

†From the Revised Standard Version Apocrypha.

Since Revelation is a record of a vision, we would not expect to find sources employed here. Yet the book contains many parallels to contemporary apocalyptic literature. The cry of the souls under the altar for vindication in Revelation 6:9-11 sounds greatly like a passage from 4 Ezra 5:35-37: "Did not the souls of the righteous in their chambers ask about these matters, saying, 'How long are we to remain here? And when will come the harvest of our reward?' And Jeremiel the archangel answered them and said, 'When the number of those like yourselves is completed.' "

Revelation 19:11-22:5 shows structural similarities to the last part of the Sibylline Oracles, book three, written more than 200 years earlier. Revelation 16:6; 17:6; and 18:24 resemble the Sibyl's prophecy that Babylon "will be filled with blood, as you yourself formerly poured out the blood of good men and righteous men" (Sib. Or. 3:311). The description of the birth of Zeus in Sibylline Oracles

3:132-141, which tells how the goddess Rhea foiled the Titans who lay in wait to devour her manchild by sending him away to be reared secretly, may have shaped the imagery of Revelation 12:4-6.

Revelation's most important extrabiblical source is a book known as First (Ethiopic) Enoch. This work influenced most of the New Testament writers, but none as much as Jude and John the revelator. Jude contains many allusions to 1 Enoch, including one extended quotation (Jude 14) taken from 1 Enoch 1:9: "And Behold! He cometh with ten thousands of His holy ones to execute judgment upon all, and to destroy all the ungodly: and to convict all flesh of all the works of their ungodliness which they have ungodly committed, and of all the hard things which ungodly sinners have spoken against Him."

No less than 20 percent of the 404 verses in Revelation show some relationship to 1 Enoch. Here is a small sample:

REVELATION*	1 ENOCH
His head and His hair were white like white wool, like snow; and His eyes were like a flame of fire (1:14).	The color of his body is whiter than snow, . . . and the hair of his head is whiter than white wool, and his eyes are like the rays of the sun (106:10; cf. 46:1).
And every created thing which is in heaven and on the earth and under the earth and on the sea, and all things in them, I heard saying, "To Him who sits on the throne, and to the Lamb, be blessing and honor and glory and do-	And He will summon all the host of the heavens, and all the holy ones above, and the host of God, the Cherubin, Seraphin, and Orphannin, and all the angels of power, and all the angels of principalities, and the Elect One, and the other

minion forever and ever" (5:13; cf. 7:11, 12).	powers on the earth (and) over the water. On that day shall they raise one voice, and bless and glorify and exalt in the spirit of patience, . . . and shall all say with one voice: "Blessed is He, and may the name of the Lord of spirits be blessed forever and ever" (61:10, 11).
Worship demons, and the idols of gold and of silver and of brass and of stone and of wood (9:20).	Worship stones, and grave images of gold and silver and wood (and stone) and clay, and those who worship impure spirits and demons (99:7).
And his tail swept away a third of the stars of heaven, and threw them to the earth (12:4).	I saw many stars descend and cast themselves down from heaven to that first star (86:3).
Blood came out from the wine press up to the horses' bridles (14:20).	The horse shall walk up to the breast in the blood of sinners (100:3).
O Lord God, the Almighty, true and righteous are Thy judgments (16:7).	Our Lord is true in all His works, and in His judgments (63:8).
And the sea gave up the dead which were in it, and death and Hades gave up the dead which were in	And in those days shall the earth also give back that which has been entrusted to it, and Sheol also shall

in them (20:13).

*From the *New American Standard Bible.*

give back that which it has received, and hell shall give back which it owes (51:1).

In both works everything in the sea dies (Rev. 16:3; 1 Enoch 101:7); the souls/spirits of the righteous dead plead for judgment (Rev. 6:9, 10; 1 Enoch 9:1-3; 22:5-7; 47:1, 2); the kings and the mighty men react in terror when they see the Lamb/Son of man sitting on His throne (Rev. 6:15ff.; 1 Enoch 62:1-10); the wicked cower before the Lord and say something about not being able to stand (Rev. 6:17; 1 Enoch 89:31); fire torments the wicked in the presence of the angels/elect (Rev. 14:10; 1 Enoch 56:8; 48:9) in a lake/river of fire and brimstone (Rev. 20:10; 1 Enoch 10:12-14; 17:5); and God/the Elect One dwells among men (Rev. 21:3; 1 Enoch 45:4; 71:16) in eternal daylight (Rev. 22:5; 1 Enoch 58:3-6).

In both we find mention of the seven angels who stand before God (Rev. 8:2; 1 Enoch 90:21; 81:5); of the angel who is in charge of the waters (Rev. 16:5; 1 Enoch 69:22; 61:10; 66:2; 60:16); of the predetermined number of slain elect (Rev. 6:11; 1 Enoch 47:4); of a great mountain burning with fire (Rev. 8:8; 1 Enoch 21:3); and of the kings of the East crossing the river Euphrates (Rev. 16:12; 1 Enoch 56:5ff.). The "great white throne" judgment scene in Revelation 20:11-15 is a pastiche of 1 Enoch 47:3; 90:20-27; and 51:1.

In the book of Revelation the expression "I saw" occurs quite frequently, as it does in Ellen White's earlier writings. Sometimes when John writes "I saw," he is paraphrasing something from the book of Enoch:

REVELATION*	1 ENOCH
After this I saw four angels standing at the four	And after that he showed me the angels of punish-

corners of the earth, holding back the four winds of the earth, so that no wind should blow on the earth or on the sea or on any tree. And I saw another angel . . . saying, "Do not harm the earth or the sea or the trees, until we have sealed the bondservants of our God on their foreheads (7:1-3).

ment who are prepared to come and let loose all the powers of the water which are beneath in the earth in order to bring judgment and destruction on all who [abide and] dwell on the earth. And the Lord of Spirits gave commandment to the angels who were going forth, that they should not cause the waters to rise but should hold them in check (66:1, 2).

After these things I looked, and behold, a great multitude, which no one could count . . . standing before the throne (7:9).

After that I saw . . . a multitude beyond number and reckoning, who stood before the Lord of Spirits (40:1; cf. 39:6b).

I saw a star from heaven which had fallen to the earth (9:1)

And again I saw . . . and behold a star fell from heaven (86:1).

And I saw an angel coming down from heaven. . . . And he laid hold of the dragon, the serpent of old, who is the devil and Satan, and bound him for a thousand years, and threw him into the abyss (20:1-3).

And I saw one of those four [angels] . . ., and he seized that first star which had fallen from the heaven, and bound it hand and foot and cast it into an abyss (88:1; cf. 10:4; 18:16; 21:6; 54:1-5).

And I saw a great white throne and Him who sat

In those days I saw the Head of Days when He

upon it. . . . And I saw the dead, the great and the small, standing before the throne, and books were opened; and another book was opened, which is the book of life (20:11, 12).

seated Himself upon the throne of His glory, and the books of the living were opened before Him; and all His host which is in heaven above and His counselors stood before Him (47:3; cf. 90:20).

*From the *New American Standard Bible.*

It is clear, then, that inspired writers demonstrate a familiarity with outside sources, not only when writing history but even when dealing with prophecy and reporting visions. However, they employ the sources critically and selectively. Although we observe many verbal parallels between 1 Enoch and the New Testament, for example, the theological differences are quite significant. The Bible writers generally borrow only disconnected phraseology, not theological ideas.

But why should inspired writers have to rely on uninspired sources for information? Why should Paul learn of the schism at Corinth not through revelation but through rumor (1 Cor. 1:11)? Why did Elisha have to ask where the borrowed ax had fallen in the water before he could make it float (2 Kings 6:6)? We might as well ask why a Christian who serves a healing God should ever have to visit the doctor. God saves His miracles for special occasions when we really need them. He does not usually do for us what we can do for ourselves, and He does not generally reveal to His prophets what they can discover for themselves. There is an economy of miracles and an economy of revelation. When Jesus miraculously fed a crowd of thousands with the meager rations from one boy's lunch, His disciples gathered up the fragments. That is God's method. Just as the apostles collected the leftovers, though Jesus could have created an abundance of fresh food if He so chose, so God's prophets assemble the fragments of truth that men have stumbled upon in ages past.

All truth is God's truth. From the prophetic standpoint, no one can own truth. It is free for the picking. Inspiration does not always consist in the revelation of previously unknown knowledge. Often it involves the selection of those items from contemporary sources that accord with the divine will so that the finished work is a product of the Holy Spirit. The fact that an inspired document makes use of the very same letters, the same words, the same phrases, and even sometimes the same paragraphs as an uninspired document should be no more shocking than the fact that the Son of God lived in the same flesh, breathed the same air, and ate the same food as did mortal men and women.

Chapter 10

Interpretation: How to Study the Bible

Since Scripture was written in a foreign language to an ancient culture and uses strange figures of speech, its meaning is not always clear to us today. Even the postexilic Jews living in Nehemiah's day had to have the Scriptures explained to them (Neh. 8:8). Christ had to interpret to His disciples the Old Testament prophecies about Himself before they could understand them (Luke 24:27). When Philip asked the Ethiopian official if he understood what he was reading from Isaiah 53, he replied, "How can I, . . . unless someone explains it to me?" (Acts 8:31).

Since the Bible needs some kind of defining or explaining, what or who is the best interpreter? Surely the best guide to any book would be its author. So the first rule of interpretation is:

Ask the Original Author—The Author of Scripture, of course, is the Holy Spirit. So never read the Bible without praying for His aid, for without the Spirit it is impossible to properly understand divine truth.

"No one knows the thoughts of God except the Spirit of God. We have not received the spirit of the world but the Spirit who is from God, that we may understand what God has freely given us. . . . The man without the Spirit does not accept the things that come from the Spirit of

God, for they are foolishness to him, and he cannot understand them, because they are spiritually discerned" (1 Cor. 2:11-14).

The Holy Spirit "will guide you into all truth. . . . He will bring glory to me by taking from what is mine and making it known to you" (John 16:13, 14), Christ promised His disciples. It is not so much intellectual ability but spiritual insight that will open to us the Scriptures.

The second rule of interpretation follows from the first. If the best guide to a book is its original author, then the most authoritative commentary on an obscure passage is another statement by the same author that says the same thing more clearly.

Let Scripture Be Its Own Interpreter—Scripture will explain itself. One verse will prove a key to unlock another. By using the cross-references in the margin of a good study Bible, and with the aid of a concordance, you can find other texts that will open up the meaning of a puzzling one.

An unabridged concordance is perhaps the most essential tool to Bible study outside of the Bible itself. The concordances found in the back of most Bibles are rather incomplete and include only a fraction of the total references. An exhaustive concordance like *Strong's* or *Young's*, or the newer NIV concordance, will list every verse in the Bible that uses a certain word. This will enable you to find other texts that employ the same word or phrase and thus interpret the verse you are studying

For example, in 2 Corinthians 5:1 Paul mentions the "earthly tent" that we live in. Whatever does he mean? Looking up the term in the concordance or consulting the marginal cross-reference will lead you to 2 Peter 1:13-15, where the writer uses the same figure of speech (actually quite common at the time) to refer to his body. The "tent" we live in is our physical body. Paul is saying that he does not want to die and be "unclothed" (2 Cor. 5:4; "naked," verse 3) from his body, but to be translated ("clothed," verse 4) without seeing death, as in 1 Corinthians 15:53, 54.

Of course, the most important clues to the meaning of an obscure passage usually appear in the verses right around the one you are studying. It is important to always

Examine the Context—The verses of Scripture are not independent oracles that we can understand in a vacuum. They form part of a sustained argument that we must interpret in their whole context.

Let us return to our previous example found in 2 Corinthians 5. What does Paul mean when he writes in verse 8 that he would like to be "away from the body and at home with the Lord"? If we have carefully examined the preceding verses—the context of the verse—we will know that he cannot be saying that he wants to die, because he has just said in verses 3 and 4 that he does *not* want to do that (be "unclothed"). Rather, he wants to be translated at the Second Coming.

Many misinterpretations of Scripture result from ignoring the context. For example, many often assume that Luke 17:34, 35, which says that on the day of the Lord one will be taken and another left, refers to a supposed secret rapture. But the preceding context says that on this day Christ's coming "will be like the lightning, which flashes and lights up the sky from one end to the other" (verse 24), and indicates that those left behind are immediately destroyed (verses 26-30). Thus the passage actually points to a glorious Second Coming, not a secret rapture.

Always read the larger passage of which your text is a part. And you will learn more if you study it in several different versions. So the next rule is:

Use Several Versions—The quickest way to get a better understanding of the sense of any passage of Scripture is to compare several modern translations of it.

For many people, reading the Bible through in a modern translation turns a drudgery into a joy. If you do all of your Bible reading in the KJV, you miss quite a bit of the meaning without even realizing it, because the archaic language of the KJV interferes with comprehension. For example, try reading Job and the minor prophets in a modern version and see how much more becomes apparent.

Translation is not an exact science. There is no one-to-one word correspondence between different languages. Most languages contain words that have no direct equivalent in another. Also, any one word can have a variety of meanings: the Hebrew word *barak* normally means "to bless," but in Job 1:5, 11; 2:5, 9 it has the connotation "to curse." It is actually easier to write a computer program to send men to the moon than to prepare one that will translate fluently. If you gave each of the world's 10 greatest translators of Chinese the same text to translate into English, you would probably end up with 10 versions that all say essentially the same thing, but in somewhat different words. By comparing all 10 translations, a reader could get a pretty accurate idea of what the original meant.

One reason for new translations is that archaeologists continue to uncover information that enables us to better understand the languages (Hebrew, Greek, and Aramaic) that the authors of the Old and New Testaments composed their various books in. More than 1,000 Greek and Hebrew words occur in the Bible only once. Until these words turned up in some ancient manuscript other than the Bible, translators could only guess at their meaning. Sometimes the KJV translators simply left such rare words untranslated. For example, the word *mazzaroth* in Job 38:32 is an untranslated Hebrew word that the KJV translators did not understand. Today we know that the word means "constellations," or "signs of the Zodiac." Likewise, in 1 Corinthians 16:22 "Anathema Maranatha" should be translated "let him be accursed. O Lord, come!" We now know that many of the superscripts, or headings, of the Psalms, left untranslated in the KJV, are the titles of tunes to which the psalms were to be sung. Modern scholars simply know more today about the languages of the Bible.

Yet another reason we need new translations is that scholars have discovered older and more accurate Greek and Hebrew texts of the Scriptures (such as the Dead Sea scrolls, Codex Sinaiticus, etc.) from which to translate. Although over the course of millennia God has guarded His Word from corruption, certain small errors of transmission have crept in. Sometimes one Greek word gets changed by a careless copyist into another word that looks almost exactly like it. For example, Revelation 22:14 in the KJV reads "do his commandments" (Greek, *entolas).* Modern translations render it "wash their robes" (Greek, *stolas).* You can see how easily a scribe could accidentally change *stolas* into *entolas* if he was copying from a smudged or otherwise defective manuscript in which the first letter of *stolas* was obscured. This sort of thing accounts for differences in many of the translations.

The more modern versions incorporate all of the latest findings of biblical scholarship, and so are often more reliable than older ones, besides the fact that they are easier to read. You will discover that hundreds of verses that were once obscure are now understandable.

Don't rely on any one translation, but compare several for a better idea of the meaning of the verse. Use the more accurate translations—those produced by a committee—such as (in order of publication) the Revised Standard Version (RSV), the *Modern Language Bible* (MLB), the *Jerusalem Bible,* the *New American Bible* (NAB), the *New English Bible* (NEB), the *New American Standard Bible* (NASB), and the New International Version (NIV), which is possibly the best translation available today. Somewhat less literal (but easier to read) is the *Good News Bible* (TEV), though Jerusalem, NAB, and NEB mentioned above are also fairly free in their translations. Versions produced by individuals—such as Weymouth, Moffatt, Goodspeed, Lamsa, Knox, Phillips, Barclay, Wuest, Beck—and *The Living Bible* are somewhat less reliable but still very useful to expose the meaning of the text. Tyndale publishes a New Testament that has eight translations in one volume.

Speaking of literal translation, it is important in reading the Bible to

Distinguish Between Literal and Symbolic Interpretation—In other words, the reader must not regard literal statements as mere symbols or figures of speech. Do not look for some mystical or metaphorical meaning when the language makes good sense interpreted literally. Most of the Bible's prose and most of its commands are meant to be taken at their plain or obvious face value.

On the other hand, the writers of the Bible often employed figures of speech just like we do. For example, we use the expressions "He kicked the bucket" or "He bit the dust" to speak metaphorically of death. The Bible also has extensive metaphorical language. The symbolic nature of biblical poetry (in the Psalms and other books), parables (in the Gospels), and apocalyptic literature (like Daniel and Revelation) is fairly obvious. It would be absurd to maintain that the dragon and the woman of Revelation 12, for example, are a literal dragon and a literal woman. Certain writers of the Bible veil their meaning in symbols and riddles in order that only the insiders, the spiritual initiates, can understand what they are saying (cf. Dan. 12:10; Luke 8:10). Those who say "I take the Bible literally" do not realize what they are saying. "Make a joyful noise unto the Lord, all ye lands." "I am the door." "Except ye eat my flesh . . ." "I have fed you with milk and not with meat." These are only a few of the figures of speech in Scripture that are not to be taken literally.

Because of problems of translation and interpretation, individual texts are sometimes subject to misunderstanding. So it is most important that we not draw doctrinal conclusions on the basis of one or two texts but gather together everything Scripture says on the subject. Before you decide what is truth,

Look at All of the Evidence—Occasionally we find paradoxes in Scripture, and people simply accept one side of the paradox and ignore the other side. For example, here is a great paradox that we have already touched upon briefly: we are justified by faith apart from works (Eph. 2:8; Rom. 11:6; Gal. 2:16; Titus 3:5). But we are judged —not just for degree of reward, but for salvation or damnation—by our works (John 5:29; Matt. 25:31-46; Rom. 2:6-11; Rev. 22:12).

Another great paradox is predestination versus free will. Whenever you find such a paradox in Scripture, don't resolve it prematurely by simply accepting one side and rejecting the other. Don't study the Bible just to prove a point. Often there is truth on both sides of an argument. Some of the great discoveries of science (such as Einstein's theory of relativity) originated from men who held two apparently incompatible theorems simultaneously and tried over the course of time to reconcile them.

Because of certain properties of logic discovered by the Czech mathematician Kurt Godel, divine truth is probably too complex to be forced into any one system (Godel found this true even of the field of mathematics). What we might consider as internal inconsistencies in the Bible are probably only hints of the complexity of God's total reality. Therefore, our next rule is:

Be Wary of Theological Systems—As long as we do not regard them as the last word on the matter, systems are useful because they impose a pattern on the data that makes it easier to understand. But they are hazardous because that pattern tends to blind us to facts that do not fit the pattern, and to prevent us from seeing the data in more useful ways.

Calvinism is an example. John Calvin was a lawyer. His orderly legal mind sought to arrange scriptural truth into a self-consistent system. Starting with a sound premise (that we are saved by faith, not by works), he then carried the premise to its logical extreme. He made it the whole sum and substance of truth, and ignored other contrasting biblical themes (such as the principle of judgment by works and conditionalism). The result was a system with five key points represented by the acronym TULIP (total depravity, unconditional election, limited atonement, irresistible grace, perseverance of the saints), which, though it contains good things, is a serious distortion of truth.

Another area in which false systems thrive is in the interpretation of Bible prophecy. In regard to the apocalyptic prophecies of Daniel and Revelation, three main systems of interpretation dominate thinking today. The preterist position (popular among modern critical scholars) says that such prophecies apply only to the time of the prophet. Their fulfillment took place in the past. Many scholars who hold this position do not believe in the inspiration of the Bible, but hold that the prophecies were simply educated guesses on the part of the prophet. In contrast, the futurist position (popular among evangelical conservatives) holds that their fulfillment is yet future, during a short period at the end of time. The third position is historicism, which finds prophetic fulfillment all down through history.

Both preterism and futurism, which originated with the Jesuit scholars Alcazar and Ribera, deny the current relevance of apocalyptic. After all, if Revelation relates only to the future or the past, not the present, then why bother with it? Fortunately, Scripture reveals both positions to be wrong.

The preterist position regards the time periods in Daniel and Revelation as consisting of literal days. But in Bible prophecy a day may stand for a year (Eze. 4:6; Num. 14:34). The 70-week prophecy of Daniel 9 and the 2300-day prophecy of Daniel 8 must stand for periods of 490 and 2300 years, not days; for only then would the 490-day/year period extend to the coming of the Messiah (Dan. 9:25), and only then would the 2300-day/year prophecy reach down to the time of the end (Dan. 8:17, 19), beyond the end of the kingdom of Greece (verses 21-23), a time yet hundreds of years away from when Daniel wrote. Daniel 8:26 and 12:4, 9 clearly say that the book of Daniel was sealed when written and was thus not meant to be understood in the present but was intended for future generations. The New Testament regarded critical parts of Daniel as still unfulfilled. According to Mark 13:14, Daniel 11:31 remained unfulfilled in Christ's day, and 2 Thessalonians 2:4 indicates that Daniel 11:36 was still future in Paul's time. Obviously, if we take the text seriously, the preterist interpretation is impossible.

Futurism, on the other hand, appears ruled out by Revelation 22:10: "Do not seal up the words of the prophecy of this book, because the time is near." Unlike Daniel, Revelation is not a sealed book applying only to the distant future. It deals at least in part with current events.

Since Daniel eliminates preterism and Revelation prohibits the concept of futurism, this leaves historicism. Although the latter system of interpretation is not currently popular among Bible scholars, it is the traditional Protestant system. It says that the prophecies of Daniel and Revelation apply to vast periods of church history, not just brief periods at the beginning (preterism) or end (futurism) of history. Of course, we must not regard even the historicist system as an absolute mold into which we must force the data. We must always remain open to new evidence.

Another principle of biblical interpretation is to recognize that

Revelation Is Progressive—If God revealed everything to His people at once, the cultural shock would be too great. Many a mother has had the following conversation with her child:

"Mommy, where did I come from?"

"You grew in Mommy's tummy."

Obviously it is not an anatomically exact answer. But it is as much as the child can understand at the moment. It would be unwise for the mother to unleash upon the child a full and explicit account of the procreative process. Just so, God reveals to His people a little at a time, leading them along to a greater understanding of His truth as they can bear it.

For example, the Old Testament does not clearly teach the doctrine of the Trinity. Surely Israel would have confused such a concept with the old polytheism that God had just weaned His people away from. Another example: we seem to find a progressive unfolding of the comings of Christ. The Old Testament makes no sharp distinction between the First and Second Advents, while the New Testament does not clearly distinguish between the Second and Third (at the close of the millennium), except in Revelation 20.

This helps us to understand some of the confusion of the disciples about the role of Jesus (cf. Acts 1:6). Even John the Baptist, though he was a great prophet, held a mistaken concept about the Messiah. He viewed Him as a temporal deliverer (*The Desire of Ages*, pp. 103, 112, 136, 137, 215, 220) who would burn up the wicked in his lifetime (Matt. 3:11, 12). When Christ did not do this, John began to have doubts about Him (Matt. 11:2, 3). Probably

John got his concept from his father, Zechariah, who prophesied under inspiration (Luke 1:67) that the Messiah would bring "salvation from our enemies and from the hand of all who hate us" (verse 71). After all, had not the Old Testament predicted that the Jewish nation's messianic king would lead them to military victory over their foes (Ps. 2; 132:17, 18; 149; Isa. 11; 61; 63:1-6; Jer. 23:5, 6; Micah 4; 5; Zech. 9)? The Baptist did not then understand the difference between the kingdom of grace and the future kingdom of glory. God did not reveal that to him.

We can also see progress in ethical and moral issues. Later revelation sometimes forbids that which earlier revelation allows. For example, in Matthew 19:8 Christ closed an Old Testament loophole that allowed for divorce on rather broad grounds, explaining that Moses permitted divorce because of the hardness of Israel's hearts, but now God wished to set a higher standard. The Old Testament did not prohibit strong drink (Deut. 14:26; Prov. 31:6, 7). Yet we do find warnings against its dangers (Prov. 20:1; 23:29ff.; Hab. 2:15). Slavery and polygamy are two other practices that God did not immediately do away with. God raises the standard a little at a time. He leads His flock gently so that they can follow. "In the past God overlooked such ignorance, but now he commands all people everywhere to repent" (Acts 17:30). Christ is always saying to His church, "I have much more to say to you, more than you can now bear" (John 16:12).

Scripture is the *living* word of God, not a dead letter. Anything that is alive grows, changes, and unfolds to reveal depths of meaning that may not be apparent on the surface. However, later revelation will not contradict earlier revelation, but is an outgrowth of it.

"The grace of Christ is illustrated by the gradual unfolding of the day, from the early morning light to the full blaze of noon. Jesus revealed to His disciples all the truth that their minds were prepared to comprehend; but the meaning of His words cannot be fully appreciated, except as the Spirit of truth illuminates the mind, and leads on to an understanding of the truth appropriate for the time" (Ellen G. White, "The Object of Christ's Teaching," *Review and Herald*, Oct. 14, 1890).

When we look at the way the New Testament quotes the Old, we discover that the New Testament writers often find a deeper meaning implicit in the words of the Old Testament than did the original writer or his readers. The Old Testament prophets did not always fully understand the message that the Holy Spirit was inspiring them to write (cf. 1 Peter 1:10-12). One prophet put it this way:

"To each [of God's servants] is granted a measure of light, adapted to the necessities of his time, and sufficient to enable him to perform the work which God has given him to do. But no man, however honored of Heaven, has ever attained to a full understanding of the great plan of redemption, or even to a perfect appreciation of the divine purpose in the work for his own time. Men do not fully understand what God would accomplish by the work which He gives them to do; they do not comprehend, in all its bearings, the message which they utter in His name. . . . Even the prophets who were favored with the special illumination of the Spirit did not fully comprehend the import of the revelations committed to them. The meaning was to be unfolded from age to age, as the people of God should need the instruction therein contained" (*The Great Controversy*, pp. 343, 344).

This is why New Testament writers sometimes seem to take liberties with the text, using the Old Testament in a very creative way. Examples are Paul's argument that the Mosaic legislation about oxen means that Christian ministers should be supported by their disciples (1 Cor. 9:9ff.), or his reasoning based on the word *seed* in Galatians 3:16. Some scholars refer to this phenomenon by the term *sensus plenior,* while others speak of typological or allegorical interpretation. At any rate, be aware that a later inspired writer may use a quotation to mean something more than what the original human author had in mind in its original context.

That does not, however, give uninspired interpreters the right to teach that Scripture has a mystical, secret, or spiritual meaning beneath the literal that we must uncover by ingenious hermeneutical devices. It is a simple recognition of the importance of

The Principle of Typological Interpretation—in which Old Testament events foreshadow spiritual realities. Thus in the New Testament *Israel* means the Christian church (Gal. 3:29; 6:16; James 1:1), the term *temple* symbolizes the body (1 Cor. 3:16), and attention no longer focuses on earthly Jerusalem but the heavenly New Jerusalem, of which the earthly is merely a type (Gal. 4:25, 26; Heb. 11:10; 12:22; Rev. 21:2). Many Old Testament figures and cultic practices hint of things to come in the gospel age. Thus King David is a type of Christ, the greater Messianic king, and the animal sacrifices of the Old Testament pointed forward to the sacrifice of Christ, the Lamb of God.

The Bible contains many things difficult to understand. Don't expect to understand everything at once. "Some passages are placed beyond the reach of human minds, until such a time as God chooses, in His own wisdom, to open them" (*Testimonies*, vol. 1, p. 377). "There are deep mysteries in the Word of God, which will never be discovered by minds that are unaided by the Spirit of God" (*ibid.*, vol. 4, p. 444). In case of perplexities, assume your understanding is at fault and lay the matter aside for later. Don't stumble over the difficulties while ignoring the great mainstream of truth. One of the most important principles in studying the Bible is:

Start With Faith; Don't Take Your Doubts Too Seriously—Many difficulties will eventually solve themselves if given the time. Active disbelief can have serious consequences. As Eve talked with the serpent in Eden (Gen. 3), she began to doubt God's word, because the evidence at the moment seemed to indicate that He had lied. After all, the Lord had said that the fruit of the tree would bring death, yet the serpent had eaten and was obviously alive—in fact, the fruit seemed to have given him the power of speech. So when the creature claimed that eating the fruit would open their eyes and give them surpassing wisdom, all the facts appeared to be on his side.

It is not safe to doubt God's Word on the basis of temporary conditions that seem to contradict it. Christ said of Lazarus, "This sickness will not end in death" (John 11:4). What must the disciples have thought, then, when Lazarus died? And why, when speedy action was so critical, did Christ dawdle so? Such questions must have seemed unanswerable for a time until the resurrection of Lazarus made all clear.

When the prima facie evidence is perplexing, faith must come into play. The scientific approach is to doubt until something is proved true. But that approach will not work with the Word of God. Instead, faith demands that we believe until a thing is demonstrated to be false. "Without faith it is impossible to please God, because anyone who comes to him must believe that he exists and that he rewards those who earnestly seek him" (Heb 11:6).

Truth is always reasonable in the long run, but at the same time it transcends reason. When the mind has reached its limit, the heart must say, "I believe." The commitment of faith to the revealed will of God is an act, not of the intellect, but of the will. Outside the flashlight beam of our knowledge lies the twilight, with all its dark questions, and beyond, in the thick darkness, is God. Faith is not a leap into the dark, as some have said, but it is a step into the twilight—a twilight that recedes before us as we take each step. We do not have all the answers, but we have the Answer, and He can be trusted.

The result of our Bible study, then, must be to

Submit and Obey—The Bible is the word of God to us. It is not merely the word of Paul to the Romans or Christ to the Jews. As such, we must study it, not out of idle curiosity, but with the purpose of putting into practice what it says. "Do not merely listen to the word, and so deceive yourselves. Do what it says" (James 1:22). The man who does this will be "blessed in what he does" (verse 25). This is why only a spiritual man can understand the Bible. The natural man will rationalize away that which applies to him. Ellen White had this problem in her day:

"When it suits your purpose," she wrote to one person, "you treat the Testimonies as if you believed them, quoting from them to strengthen any statement you wish to have prevail. But how is it when light is given to correct your errors? Do you then accept the light? When the Testimonies speak contrary to your ideas, you treat them very lightly" (*Selected Messages*, book 1, p. 43).

Scripture promises that those who decide to do God's will (John 7:17) and who choose to follow Christ (John 8:12) will find answers to their questions. Christ reveals Himself only to those who obey (John 14:21). Spiritual understanding depends on submission. Hence there is only one really good way to learn the Bible, and that is to live it.

A farmer once attempted in vain to memorize the Sermon on the Mount, until he decided to take one verse at a time and put it into practice that day. Soon he had the whole memorized.

Such practical Bible study on a regular basis is the secret of spiritual growth. Physical growth occurs naturally, without effort, as long as a person continues to eat. Likewise, spiritual growth is not strenuous effort, but feeding on God's Word. "Like newborn babies, crave pure spiritual milk, so that by it you may grow up in your salvation" (1 Peter 2:2). If you will set aside a time, a place, and a notebook, and diligently keep your daily appointment to study the Bible, spiritual transformation will naturally follow. The Bible has the power to produce the sort of character it demands.

As for your devotional life, don't feel that you have to do a specific number of verses. Instead, continue to read until you come across a passage that speaks to you—a text you can grapple with, that meets some need in your life, that answers some question, that offers some benefit. Stay with that text throughout the day, letting it run through your mind. You will soon acquire a growing understanding of truth and a growing relationship with the One whom to know is life eternal—which leads to our final rule:

Meet the Saviour—The Bible will be a dead letter to you unless you are interested in getting to know the Saviour of which it speaks. We have already discussed the error of encounter theology, which denies the possibility of objective propositional revelation. But encounter theology has a useful point. The main purpose of the Bible is not to impart technical information about God, but to bring us to an encounter with Him, to awaken within us a love for Him, and to inspire us to trust and obey Him. The Bible is more like a love letter than an encyclopedia of religious information. Jesus came to give us more abundant life (John 10:10). As we study His Word, it penetrates the heart and stands in judgment on our thoughts and motivations (Heb. 4:12) and sanctifies us (John 17:17). And as it changes us, His abundant life becomes ours.